THE ABBEY THEATRE
CRADLE OF GENIUS

W. B. YEATS

From the painting by Augustus John in the City Art Gallery, Manchester
This portrait was formerly in the collection of Lady Gregory

THE
ABBEY THEATRE

CRADLE OF GENIUS

By

GERARD FAY

LONDON
HOLLIS & CARTER
1958

First Published 1958

© COPYRIGHT GERARD FAY 1958

MADE AND PRINTED IN THE
REPUBLIC OF IRELAND BY
SEALY, BRYERS & WALKER
DUBLIN

"You have disgraced yourselves again. Is this to be an ever-recurring celebration of the arrival of Irish genius ? Once more you have rocked the cradle of genius. The news of what is happening here will go from country to country. You have once more rocked the cradle of reputation. The fame of O'Casey is born tonight."

(W. B. Yeats, in a speech from the stage of the Abbey Theatre, Dublin, on the first night of "The Plough and the Stars"—1926.)

To Alice Fay

CONTENTS

Chapter

LIST OF ILLUSTRATIONS

ACKNOWLEDGMENTS :

The illustrations in this book are reproduced by the courtesy of the City Art Gallery, Manchester ; Picture Post Library ; Bord Failte Eireann and Gabriel Fallon; The Abbey Theatre and Mr. Lennox Robinson for permission to use the drawings taken from his book 'Pictures in a Theatre,' to whom the publishers' best thanks are due.

PROLOGUE

TEN years ago, in November 1947, just before the curtain rose on the last act of Sean O'Casey's "The Plough and the Stars" at the Abbey Theatre, Dublin, a young man stood up in the auditorium and began to speak. "Ladies and gentlemen" he said "just before the show proceeds, I would like to say a few words." His was the gentlest protest ever made from the stalls of the Abbey where the more usual form of indicating displeasure has been noisy rowdiness with an unpleasant undertone of political malice. Mr. Valentin Iremonger, for he it was who stood up, had recently won the A. E. Memorial Award for a book of poems, called 'Reservations'. He was then a junior civil servant, now he is first secretary at the Irish Embassy in London. His protest went on : "When the poet Yeats died, he left behind him to the Irish nation as a legacy his beloved Abbey Theatre, then the first theatre in the world in acting, in production and in the poetic impulse of its tradition.

"Today, eight years after, under the utter incompetence of the present directorate's artistic policy, there is nothing left of that fine glory. Having seen what they did to O'Casey's masterpiece tonight in acting and production, I, for one, am leaving this theatre as a gesture of protest against the management's policy."

He then walked out of the theatre followed by several other young writers but his quiet protest reverberated in the Irish, British and American newspapers for some weeks afterwards and there was no backwardness among writers and dramatists in holding forth on "what's wrong with the Abbey?" There were plenty of different explanations and hardly anybody suggested that there was nothing wrong at all. Low salaries, high pay by film companies, the greater opportunities for good parts in London or New York were among the first points picked on. The "Irish Times" came out immediately with an explanation which was heard often : "The fault seems to lie with the board of directors, who, of late years, have forsworn the exacting standards of Yeats, Lady Gregory and the Fays, and who now,

9

it is alleged, are prepared to admit to the Abbey stage any untried novice provided his knowledge of Irish meets their requirements. Critics of the Abbey freely admit that knowledge of Irish should be a prime prerequisite for the cast of a permanent Irish-speaking theatre, but they resent bitterly the nonchalant sacrifice of the Abbey's traditional integrity on the altar of the Irish language revival."

Mr. Frank O'Connor, who had been a director of the Abbey, endorsed the protest and said that a move should be made in the government to get the subsidy withdrawn; Mr. Seán O'Faoláin said that the inspiration had departed from the Abbey and only the name was left. Cyril Cusack, an Irish actor of the first rank, trained in the Abbey, had the most damning comment of all. He said he disbelieved that it was for money that actors left the Abbey. On the other hand, "I believe it to be true that, on artistic grounds alone, few actors who are also lovers of the theatre and true followers of their tradition could be content to remain, under the present management, longer than they can help and hope."

Paul Vincent Carroll rushed in with positive suggestions. The Abbey, like any other Art Theatre, he said must be a play-wright's theatre, for great acting proceeds from great play-writing. He made a baffling reference to the censorship (which, heavy as it is on books, does not exist for the theatre in Ireland) and a much more easily understood one to the decline of the Anglo-Irish tradition "which gave Ireland an international importance in art and letters". He gave his list of remedies including "(a) Dismiss Mr. Blythe; (b) Pension off Mr. Lennox Robinson; (c) Insist on the younger school of playwrights having a training in European drama." In answer to the many attacks Mr. Ernest Blythe, the managing director, said nothing; except to give orders that Mr. Iremonger should be denied admission to the theatre if he turned up again. He did, about a year after his effective protest; and Mr. Blythe's orders were carried out.

Another director, Mr. Riobeárd O'Faracháin, did not put himself under the same rule of silence. He gave a long circum-stantial reply refuting the suggestions made about "commer-cialism", about the bad effect of the State subsidy, the treatment of new playwrights and players, and the drain on the company because of the temptations of Hollywood and the British film studios.

An organisation was founded called Friends of the Irish Theatre and among its officers was Miss Ria Mooney, who had been producing plays in Dublin for some years. In what seemed no time at all Miss Mooney was appointed a producer at the Abbey and the Directors asked her to pay special attention to experimental work which might encourage new dramatists. If that alone were regarded as the outcome of the poet's protest it was almost as effective against the stony silence of Mr. Blythe as Seanachan's sit-down strike in "The King's Threshold".

My subject is the early years of the Abbey Theatre, but I have chosen the Iremonger incident as a starting point because it illustrates many of the essential points about the Irish National Theatre which I shall attempt to establish by looking backward to its earliest motives. One is that in spite of some temporary estrangements the Dublin audience still believes the Abbey to be peculiarly its own. The money that foreign visitors pay at the box-office is welcome, but the Irish still stubbornly regard the Abbey as their special property.

A second theme that kept forcing itself forward during this and other controversies about the Abbey was the argument over whether it is a playwright's theatre or an actors' theatre. This question is not to be answered in black and white for the two types of theatre shade into each other and each is to some extent part of the other. But one distinction can be easily made. As part of the world theatre there is no doubt that the Abbey is, or at any rate was, a playwright's theatre : it is the work of the dramatists rather than the actors which has made its name known wherever the theatre is enjoyed or studied. At home in Dublin and in its repeated tours of the United Kingdom it is the acting as much as, or perhaps more than, the plays themselves which has made the Abbey's reputation stand high. Indeed it stands so high that it has sometimes been successfully exploited by youngsters of no great talent coming to London and on the strength of a few stray performances announcing themselves as "of the Abbey Theatre, Dublin." This has not always been advantageous to the Abbey and critics have murmured more than once about the apparent increase in the export of Irish ham.

Yet it is quite clear that the Abbey has built up a tradition or "school" of acting : nothing so rigid as the manner of acting imposed by, say, the Comédie Française, but recognisable and capable of being transmitted from one generation to another. One of the main points of the Iremonger protest was that this tradition had been either ignored or exploited in such a wrong direction that the actors were not doing justice to the plays, or were not allowed to do them justice. It was a grave accusation and called for a more decisive reply.

But although it seemed to be authoritatively stated at that time, ten years ago, that the Abbey Theatre was dying on its feet, somehow the patient has survived. It has happened before that the joy caused by the arrival of a new brilliant playwright has quickly turned to sorrow, and the death of the Abbey Theatre has once more been announced. Why do they never bury the corpse? The truth is that nobody is absolutely sure that the corpse will not sit up like Dan Burke of "In the Shadow of the Glen" and make the mourners regret their hasting to the wake.

Another reason for regarding all reports of the death of the Abbey as being greatly exaggerated is that nobody knows when it will next have a burst of free and profitable publicity. The British press is always ready to pounce on a likely theatrical story from Dublin and build it up with a skill in myth-making that makes even poets wonder. An example of this was the production of "The Bishop's Bonfire" in 1955. When the play was being rehearsed the word went round that it was pro-Communist and anti-Catholic. It was neither, but there was immediately an outbreak of reminiscence on the use of stink-bombs, police cordons and all the paraphernalia of theatrical rioting which since the day of "The Playboy of the Western World" has so often been thought essential to the launching in Dublin of any play about the Irish on an intellectual level above that of "Peg o' My Heart" or "Abie's Irish Rose." English newspapermen flowed into Dublin ; Irish liquor flowed into English newspapermen and within a few days the telephones were buzzing with stories of armoured cars ready to patrol the streets, police radio-cars cruising around the Gaiety Theatre; perhaps it was only the commonsense of Fleet Street that prevented readers from being told that the Irish Air Force was revving up its engines and that a document was being drafted for submission to the Security Council of the United Nations. I shall never be able to forget the expression of utter faith which illuminated the face of a bright theatrical newshawk from London as he looked me straight in the eyes and assured me he knew for a fact that "The Bishop's Bonfire" would be stopped by the audience flinging rosary beads on to the stage, if it could not be stopped in any other way.

When one of these stunt circuses descends on Dublin it brings no permanent benefit whether it is working on the latest Tennent confection, a new Sean O'Casey or on the Abbey itself. But it may sometimes perform the useful function of reminding the Dubliners themselves that they guard a great and long theatrical tradition.

The striking thing about the Abbey Theatre is the strength with which it can withstand any amount of slings and arrows, and even recover from a disaster like that of 1951 when the auditorium and backstage were gutted by fire. When the Abbey company turned up after this apparently mortal blow and began its performances at the Queen's Theatre (which have now been going on for five years) the critics and historians hardly knew where to turn for adjectives and some, I swear, spoke of "Phoenix-like arising from the flames."

There is a perfectly sound and easily explained reason for the tenacity of the Abbey Theatre and my object in this book is to make that reason clear. The theatre was founded by men and women of talent and determination and was intended to be run on lines which would ensure integrity and a certain amount of continuity. The founders also had, and needed, courage and tenacity—the courage to continue with their work in the face of quarrels and discouragements and the tenacity to keep on stubbornly with a policy once it had been laid down. These people were strong personalities and capable of imposing themselves on others. They did so and the result was that decade after decade, in spite of all manner of change and a certain amount of decay, the Abbey Theatre has hung on to its special character. Its stores of acting talent have often been wasted and dispersed but never completely lost. It has quarrelled with promising authors but the supply of new ones has never completely dried up. I believe all this happens because the theatre was built on firm foundations and it is how these were laid down that is the main part of the story I have to tell.

Books are often criticised for not achieving what their authors never set out to do ; and they are sometimes advertised as something more than the author ever intended. I should like to avoid this, so before starting to tell something of the early story of the Abbey Theatre I want to define what it is I am trying to do. This book is not the history of the Abbey. To write that is a task beyond me though I hope it will some day be done, preferably under the direction of a professional historian. It would be an excellent undertaking for the Cultural Relations Committee of the Irish Department of External Affairs to sponsor a large-scale history, and there is enough material to fill several volumes.

But I have, to some extent, used historical methods. I have studied documents and correspondence, programmes, advertisements and newspaper cuttings and learned from them things which were not self-evident at first. Letters have been the chief source of new information and for many of these I am indebted to Mrs. W. B. Yeats who lent me two large packets of her husband's correspondence. These letters have been through the hands of biographers and historians before, but the significance of some of them seems to have been missed. This applies especially to the long and vigorous series of letters from Miss Horniman which I hope will some day be published in full. These letters reveal a situation in the early days of the Abbey Theatre which has never been fully explained, partly through reluctance to conduct quarrels in public but very largely because Yeats treated much of his correspondence with Miss Horniman as private and did not always tell his fellow-directors what was in the letters.

It may be simply that he wanted to relieve them of the strain of reading Miss Horniman's long and sometimes bitter letters which came from all parts of Europe at what must have seemed a terrifying rate. She had a low opinion of Synge and of the Fay brothers—in fact her feeling about W. G. Fay might reasonably be described as loathing—and she wrote about Irish people and affairs in a way that would have horrified the faithful supporters of the Abbey Theatre. When a rival Society asked for permission to put on a play at the Abbey she wrote to the secretary:

Scene from "THE PLAYBOY OF THE WESTERN WORLD" Act 2
SARAH ALLGOOD, BARRY FITZGERALD AND ARTHUR SHIELDS

SARAH ALLGOOD

J. M. KERRIGAN

J. M. SYNGE

WILLIAM FAY

"I would willingly make a favourable arrangement with any amateur society with a reputable past and which did not pander to the curse of your country—that love of wicked politics, which teach you to hate each other so intensely, has spoiled my efforts at the Abbey Theatre. Decent people under the present circumstances are quite right in objecting to go there for they call it 'a political theatre'."

Almost her first reference to what she hoped to do at the Abbey was (in 1903) "I am so anxious to help effectually as best I may and it seems as if it were already ordained. I'll stay on here during next week to see what I am to do. Do you realise that you have now given me the right to call myself 'artist'? How I thank you!" Almost her last communication on theatre matters—eight years later—was a telegram to Yeats which read: "You have shown me that I do not matter in your eyes . . . supermen cannot associate with slaves . . . may time reawaken your sense of honour then you may find your friend again but repentance must come first."

She was not by any means consistent: when Synge was desperately ill, about a year before he died, her inquiries about him were almost tender and her anxiety clearly genuine. Yet she could contemptuously write of him "Mr. Synge wants Fay to run the show, he is too lazy to care about anything except his own plays and too cowardly to fight for the whole . . ."

In Joseph Hone's authoritative biography of Yeats there are a couple of pages mentioning Miss Horniman's objections to the Fays and other members of the company but I believe it has never been fully examined in proper perspective. It led to the final split between W. G. Fay and the directors of the Abbey (the directors having the full support of the company) and that in turn led to the Fay brothers leaving the Abbey. Of that departure P. S. O'Hegarty wrote in 1948 in a letter to the "Irish Times" : "In the case of the two brothers, Willie and Frank Fay the theatre suffered an irreparable loss, a loss which is still felt and will continue to be felt to the end of its career. Nobody that ever surveys the history of the Abbey but will reflect on the irreparable loss to it of these two men of genius, dissimilar but each essential to the proper development of the theatre." In 1903 Yeats wrote : "We owe our National Theatre

Society to W. G. Fay and his brother and we have always owed
to his playing our chief successes.''

Most writers on the Abbey have agreed that the loss of the
Fays was a serious blow, but not all would agree that it was
irreparable. Lennox Robinson, for instance, wrote to me in 1949 :
"Don't think, and now I am going to be brutal, that the Fays
were outstanding actors. The proof of the pudding is the acting.
I saw W. G. afterwards with Beerbohm Tree in 'The O'Flynn'
and many years later met him on the films in 'General John
Regan'. But in those thirty years he never established himself
as a really great actor. The Fays came in when there was an
outcry that Irish plays should be done by Irish players and they
and their company, Maire nic Shiubhlaigh and their like, were
able to fill the bill and Ireland was very proud of them. But
eventually they couldn't hold their own with Arthur Sinclair,
Fred O'Donovan, F. J. McCormick, Barry Fitzgerald and many
others. I wonder what would have happened had W. G. stuck
on, how he would have reacted to the naturalistic movement which
was inevitably coming on? These are silly questions to ask, for
they can never be answered. 'If, if, if . . .' From all the odds
and bits of letters I have read one thing seems to shine out clearly;
that the Fays, Yeats and Lady G. had very little *personal* ambition,
their ambition was for an Irish Theatre and they would sacrifice
their best friend for that. And the Fays were their best friends.''

There is much conflict of evidence and opinions about what
the Fays did or did not do at the Abbey and I hope I shall be
able to make some of the obscurities clear. It would be hardly
natural if filial pride did not show itself in what I write, but this
book is not written to advocate the idea that the Fays came
first and the rest nowhere. I believe the truth lies somewhere
between P. S. O'Hegarty's and Lennox Robinson's view. It
is not easy for me to be entirely objective on this subject but since
most of the events I write about happened fifty years ago I can,
even when my own family is concerned, look at them dispassion-
ately.

Up to the time Allan Wade's great volume of Yeats's letters
was published many of the letters I possess from Yeats to the
Fays had not been seen in print before. I sent Wade all I had
and he put several of them in his book, but there are others I

give which have not been seen before. The copies of letters of Synge's (which I quote by permission of the late Mr. Edward M. Stephens) are also in the possession of Mr. David Greene who will no doubt use some of them in his official biography of J. M. Synge.

Unfortunately no trace has ever been found of the letters Miss Horniman received about the Abbey Theatre. Her biographer Mr. Rex Pogson discovered that her literary executor never received any documents on Miss Horniman's death and he believes them to have been destroyed or distributed. This is a serious gap in the early history of the Abbey, though it is in many cases possible to read between the lines of her own letters and get a fair impression of what she was replying to. She was early on the scene and stayed some years. One of the tragedies of the early years was that she left Dublin in bitterness and disappointment, her longed-for artistic partnership with Yeats dissolved and their close friendship shaken. But the real story of the Abbey Theatre began before Miss Horniman had any notion of intervening and my story opens in 1901.

B

Chapter One

THE IDEA

IT has often baffled historians of the theatre to explain why a small country like Ireland should have provided the English-speaking world with so many dramatists of quality. The list is a long one and includes Congreve, Farquhar, Goldsmith, Sheridan, Wilde and Shaw. These men did not write for an Irish theatre and their work represents the developments of several centuries. But between 1899 and 1909 an Irish theatre was founded and developed at amazing speed and on a higher level than anybody had the right to expect. Most of its chief dramatists except O'Casey and of its cleverest players except F. J. McCormick had arrived in the first ten years and one of them, Synge, had died. It is not much of an exaggeration to say that if the Abbey Theatre had been destroyed in 1916, when it was in the line of fire of the gunboat "Helga", or if the financial troubles of the next few years had closed it, the Irish National Theatre would have left the greater part of its achievement behind it. It is always being argued whether the Abbey's chief gift to the world was the plays of Yeats, Synge, O'Casey and others or the actors trained in Dublin and exported to London, to New York and to Hollywood.

The work of the dramatist is less ephemeral than the actor's spell which he has to weave again each night and can leave behind only as the yellowing raptures of critics pasted into a press-cutting book. If he has been a strong enough influence, his name may be used for a few years to describe a certain style of acting which others have imitated. But in spite of the transience of their art it is also true to say that the Abbey was and has been an actors' theatre and that it was from an actor that the first idea of a national theatre came.

But actors and playwrights were not enough to make a national theatre. In 1904 Dublin was a "number one" town in the jargon of touring actors. It had half a dozen theatres and they all prospered in different degrees. But none of the owners of these houses would have put up the money to build yet another theatre in Dublin: indeed they tried to stop the Abbey being granted a patent to open as a full-time theatre. It was Miss Horniman who was able to stop the wanderings of the Irish National Theatre Society and set it up in a proper home. And finally Dublin was able to find—though slowly and haltingly—an audience which would support the work of the new dramatists: it was not the same audience that supported the English companies at the Gaiety or the rough dramas and farces at the Queen's. It was a new, young, and on some subjects idealistic audience more in tune with the work of Yeats, Synge and Lady Gregory than any British or American audience could ever be. "Though I wish for a universal audience" Yeats wrote in 1908 "in playwriting there is always an immediate audience also. If I am to try and find the immediate audience in England I would fail through lack of understanding on my part, perhaps through lack of sympathy. I understand my own race and in all my work, lyric or dramatic, I have thought of it. If the theatre fails I may or may not write plays—but I shall write for my own people— whether in love or hate of them matters little—probably I shall not know which it is." That was written in the only letter to Miss Horniman which Allan Wade was able to find for his immense volume and it seems to be in reply to a suggestion that he should give her the rights to his plays for English production, perhaps at the Gaiety in Manchester where she set up playhouse after leaving Dublin.

So it was the coming together of the playwrights and players, the audience and financial backer which all interacting at the right moment created the Abbey Theatre in 1904. But the roots were well grown before this happened. There were roots of two kinds —tangible ones which can be traced down through the pro- grammes of "W. G. Fay's Comedy Combination," of the Ormonde Dramatic Society, of the Irish Literary Theatre and of the Irish National Theatre Society. There were the emotional or spiritual roots which go back at least as far as Thomas Davis. The Irish language revival was one of the Abbey's roots. Yeats drew the ideas for some of his plays from legends which had been handed down in Irish, but he never attempted to learn the language. As an old man he wrote: "If Irish is to become the national tongue the change must come slowly, almost imperceptibly; a sudden or forced change of language may be the ruin of the soul. Irishmen learn English at their mother's knee, English is now their mother tongue, and a sudden change would bring a long, barren epoch."

But when Frank Fay was writing as dramatic critic in the "United Irishman" he had the Irish language very much in mind. In 1901 he wrote several important articles on "An Irish National Theatre," and in one of them he said:

"My notion of an Irish National Theatre is that it ought to be the nursery of an Irish dramatic literature which, while making a world-wide appeal, would see life through Irish eyes. For myself, I must say that I cannot conceive it possible to achieve this except through the medium of the Irish language . . . It would be well if in our Irish National Theatre we could have for our first actors well-educated native speakers, and if possible they should speak Connaught Irish . . . the people who support the Gaelic movement will support a Gaelic theatre."

Later on Frank Fay came to believe that the language revival was tending to make the people illiterate in two languages instead of in one only. He was scornful of the idea that the later Abbey could ever become a Gaelic theatre and it is easy to guess what he would have thought of the theatre's being called "Amharclann na Mainistreach" and even easier to imagine what he would have said about the rule that aspirants to the permanent company of the Abbey must now be able to act in Irish. The audience does not get many chances (and does not seem to want many) of judging the Gaelic talents of the company but some Abbey acting nowadays, when English is the language, makes it perfectly clear what Yeats meant when he wrote ". . . . a sudden change would bring a long barren epoch."

Although it was a doctrine especially supported by Lady Gregory that the whole national theatre movement sprang from a nationalist urge among a group of authors, the "United Irishman" articles show that some of the actors had the same urge and expressed it first. At the time they were published Edward Martyn had not yet written his "Plea for a National Theatre in Ireland" (Samhain, October, 1901) though Yeats, Lady Gregory and Moore had been actively at work on the Irish Literary Theatre.

It is fifty-six years since these articles were written and I doubt if anybody has ever looked them up since, so I propose to quote at some length from them.

Perhaps it is necessary to remind readers of today that the "United Irishman" was started in 1848 by John Mitchel, author of the "Jail Journal" and one of those who inspired the Fenian movement. He was transported to Van Diemen's Land soon after the paper began but he escaped to America where he made himself as much a nuisance to the Union government as he had been to the British. In 1900 the resurrected "United Irishman" was being edited by Arthur Griffith who, to begin with, was well disposed towards the national theatre but later on became a bitter enemy of the Abbey.

The first article, May 4th 1901, began by noting George Moore's announcement that the Irish Literary Theatre would not produce any play that year until there was a suitable English company available at one of the Dublin theatres to take on the production. The plays chosen were Moore's "Diarmuid and Gráinne" (in which Yeats collaborated) and Douglas Hyde's "Casadh an tSúgáin ("The Twisting of the Rope"). As it turned out the short play in Irish was directed by W. G. Fay who took over when it proved too much for George Moore.

" I would prefer " Frank Fay wrote " to see a theatre inaugurated here that would abolish English completely and conduct its operations outside the uncongenial atmosphere of an English commercial theatre.

"What I want to know is why the conductors of the Irish Literary Theatre who pooh-pooh the ordinary English commercial theatre cannot entrust the performance of their plays dealing with Irish subjects to a company of Irish actors. I know, of course, that I shall be told there are no Irish actors; that the Irishman who goes on the stage must sink his individuality and his accent as much as it is possible for him to do, otherwise he will not rise above the class of stuff that Mr. Whitbread is in the habit of presenting to his patrons . . . [at the Queen's].

"It is manifestly the duty of those who will benefit by the Irish Literary Theatre plays to train up a company of Irish actors to do the work they want. Antoine did it in Paris and trained himself as well, for he was originally a clerk, and had been refused admission to the Conservatoire . . .

"Where is the use of using the title "Irish" Literary Theatre if we have to get English actors because we are too lazy to train up Irish ones? It is not long since I heard a rumour that even Dr. Hyde's play was to be handed over to the Saxon who was to be taught to parrot the lines, but I imagine the strength of the Irish language movement has prevented the committee from risking such a dangerous experiment.

"The curious part of the matter is that the actor to whom 'Diarmuid and Gráinne' has been entrusted, and who is much boomed as a Shakespearean actor, cannot speak 'To be or not to be,' or the speech of Hamlet to the Players without leaving out or interpolating words. . . . How Mr. Yeats whose fastidiousness with regard to speaking is well known, will like hearing his lines mauled by these people is a matter about which I am curious" The actor he was so hard on was F. R. Benson, later Sir Frank to his audiences and "Pa" Benson to the whole theatrical profession. Harcourt Williams, Henry Ainley and Matheson Lang were in his company. Frank Fay became a friend of Frank Benson's, but never an admirer. The article ends with an ambitious appeal:

"Cannot the committee of the Irish Literary Theatre build a hall about the size of the stage of the Queen's Theatre? There they could act their plays with the certain knowledge that so long as they appeal to Irish sympathies they will get the support of the immense and delightful audiences who are supporting the movement which is reviving our music . . ."

Later in May the "United Irishman" printed the two articles entitled "An Irish National Theatre". The first is the more memorable because it contains many original ideas and precise suggestions. The second was mainly a description of what had been done in setting up the Norwegian National Theatre in Bergen. After the assertion that the National theatre was inconceivable except in the Irish language he continued:

"I have read and seen many plays purporting to be Irish
written in English, but save that they told an Irish story the
only real distinction was in the employment of a dialect more
or less accurate, generally less. It is the old saying over again,
No language, No nation, and consequently no drama. English
is not our language; it is foreign to our nature and weighs us
down . . . Now that the Gaelic movement is so large, the time is
ripe, if not for an Irish National Theatre, at least for the nucleus
of one in the shape of the frequent performance of plays in the
Irish language. We have now several very capable Anglo-
Irish dramatists, but the Irish Literary Theatre is their proper
place, unless they will take the trouble, as many people of much
less eminence have done, of learning to express themselves in
Irish."

He ended with some comments on the difficulty of attracting
the right people to do this acting, partly because in Ireland
". . . there exists a scathing contempt for the 'play-actor'; he is
not considered respectable, and we have been long suffering
from an acute attack of respectability."

The second of this pair of articles mentions an ideal director
for an Irish National Theatre—"I need not say I refer to Dr.
Douglas Hyde, in whom, perhaps, we shall one day also find a
National dramatist. Mr. Edward Martyn and Mr. Yeats would
also be very valuable in connection with such an institution but
their usefulness as dramatists would be considerably hampered
by their work being done in English instead of in Irish . . . Dr.
Hyde would be qualified to do what few others in Ireland could
do: he could instruct the actors of an Irish National theatre in
the proper method of declaiming verse and prose written in our
national language, which would be a vitally important matter."

The next "United Irishman" article by Frank Fay on the
National Theatre theme was a review of "Diarmuid and Gráinne"
and "Casadh an tSúgáin" produced at the Gaiety Theatre on
21st October 1901, the first play acted by Mr. Benson's company,
the second by members of the Gaelic League, including, as
Lennox Robinson discovered (there were no names on the programme) the Misses O'Kennedy, O'Donovan and Sullivan and
Mr. Tadhg O'Donoghue. The review began ecstatically: "Monday evening was a memorable one for Dublin and Ireland.

The Irish language has been heard on the stage of the principal metropolitan theatre, and 'A Nation Once Again' sung within its walls, and hope is strong within us once more." He found "Diarmuid and Gráinne" a good play, but could hardly bring himself to mention the acting by the English company. "All through the play the English voice grated on one's ear, and the stolid English temperament was equally at variance with what one wanted. The actors did not act the play as if they believed in it . . . I do not therefore intend to say anything about the interpretation, because the play was simply not interpreted at all . . ."

Ecstacy returned in the comments on "Cásadh an tSúgáin" which he found "wonderfully well acted, considering that those who played in it had never been at such work before." He closed with a "high compliment" to his brother W. G. Fay for having produced the play ". . . without a hitch, with absolute novices for actors."

Before returning the "United Irishman" cuttings to their seldom disturbed volume in my father's archives there is one more article to be quoted.

On October 26th, 1901, still hammering away at the National Theatre theme, he wrote that he was glad to see that "Mr. Yeats has at last cut himself adrift from the so called 'upper' classes and that he recognises that an Irish Theatre would be worthless if it were to be in the hands of people who could in any way prevent it from acting outspoken plays.

"Municipal aid is suggested, but it is difficult to see how municipal aid could be availed of in Dublin. People who present addresses to the rulers of England would certainly not permit our money which unfortunately they control to be devoted to an institution whose principal object would be to act plays holding up to opprobrium England and her methods. They might subsidise harmless institutions; but an Irish Theatre, to be worthy of the name, should be quite fearless and fetterless, and be able to say what it wants about anyone or any class of people. A Municipal Theatre would almost certainly fall into the hands of the wrong people . . . an Irish National Theatre will not come at once: its evolution will be gradual . . . We shall find our actors among Cumann na nGaedheal and among the Inghinidhe na hEireann or others who, possessing the histrionic temperament are not afraid to use it in the service of Ireland."

During the summer in which these articles were written Frank Fay started his long correspondence with W. B. Yeats. For years he deluged Yeats with letters, press cuttings and memoranda all of which were designed, in one way or another, to instruct Yeats in points of theatrical history or to learn from him what ought to be the correct relationship between actor and poet. Yeats's replies show an important part of his character—that once he had started to take an interest in the theatre (it might well have been some other subject) he would not rest until he had mastered its technical side, at any rate to his own satisfaction. He was forever probing into the reasons why things ought to be done in one way rather than in another. He found it useful to have confirmation from Frank Fay's studies of theatrical history for theories about speech, gesture, costumes, scenery and music.

Yeats re-wrote constantly as any reader of successive editions of collected works can see. When he was first writing his plays he sent long letters of instruction (usually to one of the Fay brothers) about how he wanted the parts played.

An example of how he kept his eye on detail is a letter from Coole in 1902 in which he performs by remote control some of the functions of producer as well as of author. It deals with three plays. He first refers to difficulties in "Kathleen ni Houlihan"—difficulties from the actor's point of view. One, he says, is obviously a misprint and "no doubt there is confusion between the names Peter and Patrick in the other passage you speak of". He says Lady Gregory is trying to find the air of "There's Broth in the Pot", that he will send sketches of costumes for "The Hour Glass" and that he encloses "some Latin words which will do for the wise man's prayer."

"Digges should not make up too old", he continues. "The wise man is a man in the full vigour of life. I hear from Mr. Quinn that he read the part very finely and you yourself I hear played very excellently. Quinn was very much struck. I should like however to hear how 'The Pot of Broth' goes. Let the fool's wig, if you can, be red and matted."

One of Yeats's difficulties in Ireland was that he often found himself caught in a moral cross-fire between people of his own class, who were Protestants, and Catholic nationalists who suspected him because of his Rosicrucianism, theosophy and other mystic pursuits. The best guide to this side of his character is Richard Ellman's book "Yeats the Man and the Masks". In it he quotes a declaration of the poet's which was the sort of thing that upset people of all religions.

"I believe" he said "that literature is the principal voice of the conscience and that it is its duty age after age to affirm its morality against the special moralities of clergymen and churches and of kings and parliaments and peoples . . . I have no doubt that a wise ecclesiastic, if his courage equalled his wisdom, would be a better censor than the mob, but I think it better to fight the mob alone than to seek for a support one could only get by what would seem to me a compromise of principle."

In the earliest days of the Irish National Theatre Yeats was evidently in a more pliant mood. His contempt for "the mob" was kept under control, though no doubt it was later fanned by Miss Horniman. But as a former member of the Irish Republican Brotherhood he could hardly have shared her contemptuous dislike of Irish nationalists. When Allan Wade called on her in 1908 during his work on the first bibliography of Yeats she remarked "I referred him to Mrs. MacBride [Maud Gonne] for a paper published in Paris and to Lady Gregory for the gutter journal "United Ireland". Being in Dublin it would be easy to go through the files at the Sinn Fein office and that miserable little rabbit would not dare refuse permission for *her* to look through them."

But the "gutter journal" and the "miserable little rabbit", its editor Arthur Griffith, played an important part in the future of the Abbey Theatre, for it was they who brought W. B. Yeats and Frank Fay into direct contact and made a junction of the different lines being followed by the Fay brothers and the other pioneers of the growing Irish theatre.

"My Dear Griffith," Yeats wrote in July 1901, "My little play 'The Land of Heart's Desire' has had so far as I can make out a great success in America. Lady Gregory a few days ago got the idea that you might perhaps write a paragraph on it if she sent you the material. She has copied out as you will see by the enclosed a great many press notices, in which you may find something to quote. She thinks it will help our Theatre as it will make people take me more seriously as a dramatist. However that may be I would like some little record in some Irish paper and in your paper by preference. I always write for my own people though I am content perforce to let my work come to them slowly.

I am just starting a little play about Cuchullin and Concobar partly I dare say encouraged by this American success. The seeming impossibility of getting my work sufficiently well performed to escape mere absurdity had rather discouraged me."

The days of discouragement were very nearly over because Griffith passed this letter on to his dramatic critic who also reviewed theatrical books and did weekly notes on various Gaelic and national activities which came very roughly under the theatrical heading—recitals, feiseanna or Gaelic festivals, concerts and so on. He duly did his notice of the book and before it was published sent Yeats a long letter on modern and 18th century methods of declaiming verse on the stage. Towards the end of it he wrote: "I hope I have not said anything in what I wrote in 'U.I.' that you consider puts you in a false light. I love that little play and tried to show it in what I said, but know how inadequate I am to deal with your work. I wrote in the hope of sending others to read the play . . . My only regret is that your work is not for the *Irish* language, which was *made* for dramatic utterance." The letter finishes with a short dissertation on English and Irish vowel sounds, the Comédie Française playing Greek tragedies in the Roman theatre at Orange and whether or not the Greeks intoned their speeches. "You see how I become diffuse on this subject," he ends "but as you are deep in it you will pardon me."

Yeats was staying at Lady Gregory's home and his reply (on August 1st, 1901) was headed "at Coole Park, Gort, Co. Galway:

Dear Mr. Fay,

I was altogether pleased with your article on "The Land of Heart's Desire" in the 'U.I.' I am very glad too that you are going to say something about the Gaiety Theatre dread of naming either Moore or myself. I am more surprised at Hyland's stupidity than at his fear . . . He has been very nervous from the start and even feared that doing a play by us might keep people away from Benson's Shakespeare performance. The ordinary theatre-going person in Dublin, of the wealthier classes dislikes our movement so much that Hyland has something to say for himself. An esteemed relative of my own told me a while back that Douglas Hyde had said in a speech that "he hoped to wade through Protestant blood," and would hardly believe me when I denied it. They look on us all in much the same way—Literary Theatre, 'Gaelic League' are all one to them . . . I wish very much that my work were for the Irish language for many reasons. I hope to collaborate with Hyde in a little play shortly. I shall be in Dublin for your performances in 'The Antient Concert Rooms.' I see by the paper that they begin on the 26th."

This exchange of letters makes two important points in the pre-history of the Abbey Theatre. It establishes the contact between Yeats and the Fays. It was also the beginning of a correspondence which disposes of hints made in some writings on the early players that the Fays and their companions were a company of rude mechanicals who became important to the Irish theatre only after they had met the refining influences of Yeats, Lady Gregory and Miss Horniman.

A difference of education existed, certainly. Yeats and W. G. Fay had both had an interrupted secondary education. Neither went to a university. Frank Fay had no secondary education except what he gave himself, but that was extensive and included an excellent knowledge of French, of Pitman's shorthand, elementary physics and chemistry, electricity and magnetism. In his twenties, which was the decade 1890-1900 he added an extraordinarily detailed knowledge of the English and French theatre, both technical and literary. On any theatrical subject the Fays spoke to Yeats as an equal, that is after he had studied sufficiently to catch up with what they had learned while he had been deep in theosophy and the Order of the Golden Dawn.

Frank Fay worked away at Yeats as though he were preparing him for an examination. He never moved far from the question of the relationship between the actor and the poet and of what the poet should demand of the actor in declamation, elocution or just plain speech.

This passionate interest in the spoken word was the strongest link between Frank Fay and Yeats. It persisted through the quarrels of later years. It was their first link and almost their last, for it was not long before Frank Fay died that Yeats asked him to create a character in a private performance of one of his later Noh plays produced in the drawing-room of 82 Merrion Square, Dublin.

Their discussions on verse-speaking led to Yeat's abandoning some extravagant ideas he had picked up on the subject. They led to Yeats's having Frank Fay's voice in mind when he wrote some of his plays (the dedication of "The King's Threshold" is to Frank Fay ". . . and his beautiful speaking in the character of Seanchan"). But this early relationship between the poet and the actor also led to some of the jealousies which from the very beginning afflicted the Irish theatre movement, making it unduly fissile and liable to hiving off of little cliques as one split followed another.

In the formative years, though, there was no doubt about Yeats's being willing to work closely with and even to be led to some extent by the Fays. This did not always please Lady Gregory who, even then, was so watchful of Yeats's fame that it seemed to hurt her if he had to share credit with others.

Chapter Two

LAYING FOUNDATIONS

GEORGE MOORE began chapter seven of "Vale" with the question "But who is Frank Fay? the reader asks." His reply was just about half accurate, which was pretty good by his own standards of reporting. "In the days of 'Diarmuid and Gráinne' " he explained "he was earning his living as a shorthand writer and typist in an accountant's office, and when his day's work was over he went to the National Library to read books on stage history. His brother Willie was a clerk in some gas-works, and painted scenery when his work was over, and both brothers, whenever the opportunity offered, were ready to arrange for the performances of sketches, farces, one-act plays in temperance halls. But 'Box and Cox' did not satisfy their ambitions; and the enthusiasm which 'The Twisting of the Rope' had evoked brought Willie Fay to my house one evening to ask me if I would use my influence with the Gaelic League to send himself and his brother out, with a little stock company, to play an equal number of plays in English and Irish."

If this interview took place Willie Fay seems to have forgotten it completely. But might it not be Mr. Moore's memory which was defective? In his previous chapter rhapsodically describing how he acted as *régisseur* for Dr. Hyde's little play Moore was so carried away that he forgot to mention that it was Willie Fay who finished the job of producing "The Twisting of the Rope". Moore's odd methods as a stage manager got him nowhere with Irish amateurs and in the end he threw in his hand, asking Willie Fay to take over who had only a year before that directed the first public performance of a play in Gaelic—"An Tobar Draoidheachta" ("The Magic Well") by Father Dineen.

When he said that W. G. Fay was "a clerk in some gasworks" it seems clear that Moore had lodged somewhere in his unreliable memory an image of Antoine, founder of the Théâtre Libre in Paris. He was a clerk in the gas works. Willie Fay was an electrician by trade and had been doing well at it before he gave up his regular job in 1904 to supervise the building of the Abbey Theatre for Miss Horniman. Frank Fay, who started as a clerk in the offices of an accounting firm called Craig, Gardner had become secretary to one of the partners by the time he left to be a professional actor. But he had at the time Moore writes of done a great deal more than go to the library to study theatre history.

In the previous ten years he had often been left alone in Dublin to carry on the various amateur dramatic societies in which he and his brother were the senior partners. They both had the disease of stage-madness in its most severe form and like many young men in their twenties they got little encouragement from their parents. In fact for a while they were under such disfavour that they did not even act under the name of Fay but took on the stage names of W. G. Ormonde and Frank Evelyn. This lasted several years.

The earliest records of their work that I have been able to find are programmes of 1891 when Willie was 19 and Frank 21. At the Father Mathew Centenary Hall in Dublin the Leinster Choral Union was offering "Two Grand Musical and Dramatic Entertainments." Part Three consisted of an overture . . . "After which a Screaming Sketch will be performed by W. G. Ormonde's Combination." The sketch was not given a name but the characters were Flipper played by Mr. Frank Evelyn, Nobbler and Jim by Mr. W. G. Ormonde and Lodger by Mr. James Marshall.

In 1892 and 1893 the company and its repertory grew. The name "Ormonde Dramatic Society" was adopted (the family lived in Ormond Road, Dublin). By 1897 W. G. Fay's name began to appear on the programmes though Frank remained Evelyn until he played the name part in "Paddy Miles, or The Limerick Boy." When they dropped their stage names they also seemed to become much busier though there is not much evidence that W. G. Fay prospered as a result of this announcement which used to appear on some of the programmes: "W. G.

Above—THE ABBEY THEATRE before the fire

Below—Scene from "THE PLOUGH AND THE STARS" Act 2
ERIC GORMAN, F. J. MCCORMICK, SHEILA RICHARDS, EILEEN CROWE
AND JOSEPH LINNANE

THE HALL
where Dramatic History was made

THE FAMOUS GONG
which announces the
rising of the curtain

FRANK FAY

F. J. McCORMICK

Fay, having had long experience in the Theatrical Profession, is at liberty to attend Amateurs. First class fit-up and Scenery for Hire. Terms Moderate."

It was not from any deep conviction about teetotalism that the Fays attached themselves to a total abstinence organisation, which they did in about 1898. It was because the various club-rooms and "Coffee Palaces" needed a steady flow of entertainment and had roughly equipped stages. The Fays and their companies played frequently in these places and were able to make the experiments by which they taught themselves and others a great deal of simple acting skill. The material was crude, true enough, but it was mainly farcical comedy, one of the most difficult of theatrical mediums, and in attempting to master this no group of amateurs could fail to teach themselves a lot. But they never stood on their dignity; a gap in the programme could always be filled by a comic song; and one of the singers was Fred Hanna, who later became the best-known bookseller in Dublin.

In 1899 there were changes of name and of cast. Mr. J. Dudley Digges first appeared both as reciter and as actor. The company was called "Mr. W. G. Fay's Celebrated Variety Co." in January and "Mr. W. G. Fay's Comedy Combination" in May. The stage names "Evelyn" and "Ormonde" disappeared altogether.

The brothers had taught themselves and others a simple acting technique but for some time their minds, especially Frank's, had been running on more serious matters than farces put on at Coffee Palaces. Frank read more than theatrical history. He took long notes on everything he could find about the Théâtre Libre in Paris, the National Theatre in Bergen and the Independent Theatre in London. His files of the pre-Irish Literary Theatre period are full of William Archer, Shaw and Ibsen. His admiration for the technical accomplishment of "old fashioned" acting was blunted by impatience with its crudeness and with the worthlessness of the plays chosen by almost every English speaking theatre.

Shakespeare and 18th century comedy would have satisfied him, or some repertory based on the "advanced" drama of the mid-'nineties. If there had been a Poel in Dublin, or a Grein or a Granville Barker, if there had been a chance to act in a classical or advanced company Frank Fay would probably have

C

taken it. But there was no such chance in Dublin at the time. Therefore, with his brother, he decided it was time to find something better to do with their energies and talents and their Ormonde Dramatic Society. In his own account, given to an Irish Society in New York in 1908 he explained how his writing for the "United Irishman" brought him in touch not only with Mr. Yeats but with the Inghinidhe na hEireann—the Daughters of Erin—a revolutionary society in which Maud Gonne was a leader. He was asked to help the society in putting on some tableaux of Irish historical subjects:

"In this work I had the assistance of my brother who had spent some seven years on the regular stage playing in all sorts and conditions of plays. These tableaux having proved very successful, the Daughters of Erin decided on giving a similar entertainment later on in the same year, 1901, with the addition of a play or two. The production of these plays was put into my brother's hands and to act in them he had the assistance of an amateur company which he had organised . . At the performances of these plays Mr. Yeats was present and said to me one evening at the fall of the curtain "I like the grave acting of your company".

Maud Gonne claimed that Inghinidhe na hEireann was one of the first societies for open revolutionary work and that it almost stopped enlistment for the British army in Dublin, so that Queen Victoria had to come over to stimulate it again.

"Crowds gathered once if she but showed her face,

And even old men's eyes grew dim. . ."

These were two of the many notable lines in which W. B. Yeats recorded Maud Gonne's beauty. As a politician (but never quite a stateswoman) as an actress and as a seeker after mystic "truths" she ran through his life, a recurrent and disturbing theme. She was a daughter of the Protestant ascendancy but was never orthodox in her own religion and put it aside to follow the strange paths of the "Order of the Golden Dawn" into which Yeats had strayed under the influence of MacGregor Mathers after his explorations of Madame Blavatsky's theories and of theosophy. It was in the same magic circle that Yeats met one of the other women who was to mean so much to him—Miss Annie Elizabeth Fredericka Horniman. Later in life, having devoted herself unselfishly to Irish Republicanism and married one of its martyrs, Major MacBride, Maud Gonne became a Catholic. By 1901, when both Yeats and Maud Gonne had resigned from the Irish Republican Brotherhood, the Daughters of Erin was only one of many societies engaged in planning rebellion against England, directly or indirectly. The Gaelic Athletic Association, the Celtic Literary Society and others provided excellent cover for revolutionary work while carrying on ostensibly doing something else. There were some who hoped that the Irish National Theatre would develop in the same way. The fact that it did not caused one of the earliest and most serious crises in the Abbey Theatre. But all this was some time ahead. The Daughters of Erin brought Yeats and the Fay brothers into direct touch; the tableaux vivants probably did little for the freedom of Ireland ("Marie Kileen, one of the executive . . . a dark girl, looked very beautiful as Dark Rosaleen" Maud Gonne remembered) but they assembled the most important figures in the early days of the national theatre, for A. E. (George Russell) was with Yeats at the Antient Concert Rooms that night, and Lady Gregory was there too.

This was the Autumn festival which Inghinide na hEireann got up "to discourage . . . the attending of vulgar English entertainments at the theatres and music-halls" and by Spring they were helping to put on the first plays of the dramatic revival, quickly succeeding where the Irish Literary Theatre had slowly failed. The society was given yet another new name "W. G. Fay's National Dramatic Company," the stage was in the hall of St. Teresa's Total Abstinence Association, Clarendon Street, and some of the players were carried over from the Ormonde Society. The Fays had already begun to develop ideas on acting in a style quite different from that of "The Limerick Boy" or "The Colleen Bawn" (which they had produced on the same stage, but not acted in). "We thought it was time" Frank Fay said "to make the Irish accent and idiom in the speaking of English a vehicle for expression of Irish character on the stage and not for the sole purpose of providing laughter."

Up to now, in spite of Frank's enthusiasm for the Irish language and his patriotic contempt for England the Fays had only one passion in life—the theatre. They brought their ideas and their theatrical skill, learned over ten years of hard work, into a literary and political world where there was much less singleness of purpose. Yeats had several passions including the Golden Dawn, the promotion of his own fame as a poet, and Maud Gonne. Maud Gonne had a passing interest in the theatre and would once have gone on tour as leading lady in "Heartsease" (a version of 'Adrienne Lecouvreur') if she had not had a haemorrhage of the lungs. Her breach of this contract had one consolation for her—"If I had gone on the stage it would have taken me away from Ireland."

But before giving up the theatre for politics Maude Gonne played in "Kathleen ni Houlihan". The greater excitement before the curtain went up was all about "Deirdre" because A. E. had not written a play before and the third act had had to be almost squeezed out of him by the Fays. He was giving it to them as a reward for their good work with the Daughters of Erin and they brought to it all they had learned. They also brought some of the most accomplished members of their Society —Dudley Digges, P. J. Kelly and C. Caulfield. The Daughters provided Maire Quinn and Maire Walker, who was the first to use her name in Irish on any National Theatre programme. She appeared as Maire Nic Shiubhlaigh and in her book "The Splendid Years" has given a full and eloquent account of this famous production. Padraic Colum was in the cast too, though at that time he still spelt his name Colm or Columb or even occasionally Collumb.

In spite of the anticipations for "Deirdre" the more important piece turned out to be "Kathleen ni Houlihan" which Yeats had written in a hurry and finished with Lady Gregory's help. The audiences were as large as St. Teresa's Hall could hold (about 300). Perhaps some of them came more to support total abstinence than to launch a national theatre, but at least they came. Edward Martyn described "Kathleen ni Houlihan" as "a silly little play" but he was alone in the opinion. Many of the young men and women were watching a nationalist play for the first time, though the patriotic message was presented only in parable form. The last lines of the play were the first memorable words of the new Irish national drama:

> Bridget (to Patrick) :—Did you see an old woman going down the path?
> Patrick :—I did not, but I saw a young girl and she had the walk of a queen.

Nobody remembered much about "Deirdre" though Willie Fay said the audience liked it. It was mainly a working-class audience he said: "They were enthusiastic. Their joy was a delight to see. They loved the patriotic sentiment of Kathleen while the romance of Deirdre was so beautiful and novel that they hardly knew how to express their feelings." They expressed their feelings in the only way that matters to actors and actresses; they clapped and cheered and remembering the success later on Yeats wondered if anybody in that audience, and others which saw "Kathleen", had been inspired beyond what the dramatist usually hopes for:

> Did that play of mine send out
>
> Certain men the English shot?

These three nights in Clarendon Street touched many imaginations, both on the stage and in the audience. The prospect of these performances had excited Frank Fay two months earlier when he wrote to Yeats "Your little play has reached us safely through Mr. Russell, and it is now in rehearsal. We are all delighted that Miss Gonne is to act Kathleen and I look for a great success for all of us. If we achieve it, I think it will result in our endeavouring to give more frequent performances of such plays by Irish authors as we can get. I may mention that our company for 'Deirdre' includes two poets and that one of these has written several little plays and we hope to produce one for him when he is a little stronger in technique". One of the poets was Padraic Colum who took almost two years to strengthen his technique sufficiently for "Broken Soil" to be produced.

Frank Fay asked Yeats for costume sketches and hoped to hear whether "you wish anything special done with the play."

Was there any music for Miss Gonne to use for the songs? He was already thinking ahead of this production to the possibility of a permanent company and was struck by the difficulty of finding a hall. He described St. Teresa's as the only adequate one in Dublin, though he said its stage could have done with being twice as large and it had no dressing rooms. He thought there would be no shortage of plays but he was certain that they could not be "outspoken" unless the society had its own hall.

But the success was not allowed to turn the practically minded brothers into mere dreamers. A week afterwards Frank Fay wrote to Yeats mentioning that all the papers had been very good to the actors and, for a change, had after ten years taken their work seriously though "I fear that had we not been associated with your play and Deirdre we would have waited another ten". But in an article about the plays Yeats had referred to "crudity" in the acting. There seemed to be a chance here to discover something that might be put into practice: "What I would like to ask you to point out is what you consider our defects and errors of execution which you refer to in your note. You certainly say the right thing when you say we cannot have too much practice, though I don't know where it is to come from yet. I hear that the 'Leader' says the shillings of the Gaelic Leaguers were largely in evidence; that is not true. If we had to depend on the League, we'd have had another Horse Show week. The majority of them cannot follow a play in Irish but they use their 'no politics' cry as a defence for not supporting us though we are paving the way for the play in Irish."

A few days later he wrote again complaining that Yeats would not candidly say what he thought were the "crudities" but seeming thankful that Yeats had not given "unqualified praise, as the 'Independent' did for instance which said that the acting was perfect." On the subject of a permanent home or a hall to play in more regularly he remarked that he thought St. Teresa's would not again be available and that they could have the Father Mathew Hall "if we cared to comply with certain conditions which we could not think of accepting."

"There is left the large Concert Room in the Rotunda which you get with a bare platform and curtains but without gas for £4 a night and during the winter it is continually in use . . .

In the discussion at the Contemporary Club there was too much reference to a theatre; all that is wanted is a hall about half as large again as Teresa's." His brother Willie was more optimistic, saying that the difficulties would be got over as they had been before and Frank was certainly cheerful about plays. Apart from having Colum at work he had been given a completed play by James Cousins, "The Racing Lug". "I am not going to say of it" he wrote "as was said of Hyde's play that it is as good as any one-act play of de Banville or de Musset, but I have 15 years' experience as a playgoer and I have never seen a one-act play that could touch this. It is a bit of life. James Cousins was the second of the "two poets" in the Deirdre cast. He played one of the sons of Usna, using the stage name of H. Sproule. Another of the cast, Fred Ryan, was busy finishing a two-act play, to be called "The Laying of the Foundations" and to be staged in 1902 in the first production of the Irish National Theatre Society.

Although it cannot have been clear at the time the presence of these three would-be dramatists in the acting company (and each of them finished his play and saw it produced) was an early trend which soon reversed itself. Later on, although they worked closely together, the actors and the playwrights increasingly became two different communities. There was even a tendency which continued for many years (for example through the work of Lennox Robinson and Sean O'Casey) for the writers to be Protestants and the actors Catholics. Perhaps this was entirely accidental but at times it was useful to enemies of the Abbey Theatre to be able to say that the directors were not Catholics and that the money came from an Englishwoman. Even in the earliest days there was a sign of inner tension on grounds of orthodoxy. Edward Martyn was the wealthiest of the Irish Literary Theatre's active supporters and among the hardest workers for a Dublin version of the Independent Theatre. One of the earliest historians of the Abbey, Ernest A. Boyd, described Martyn's aim as "to write for the existing London theatres open to literary plays and not to found a theatre for the special purpose". Martyn was a powerful and cultivated critic who knew far more about the theatre at that time than Yeats did. He vigorously attacked, on grounds of technique, the production of Deirdre and Kathleen ni Houlihan. He was the strongest Ibsenite of the early years in the Abbey's life, but unlike Yeats, Lady Gregory and Synge he was a Catholic and his earliest quarrel had been about the production (in 1899 by the Irish Literary Theatre) of "The Countess Cathleen" which offended some of the devout and some of the clergy—who were never the best friends of the theatre in Ireland.

Frank Fay, not having at first mentioned Martyn's attack in his letters to Yeats came to it in the end. He was not surprised by what Martyn had to say and he could see clearly how deep was the division of ideas between Yeats, A.E. and the actors on one side and Martyn on the other. "If *we* succeed" he wrote "the acting of *his* plays in Ireland will be difficult, and it is only natural that he should try to fight for his own hand. But he has only damned himself because if he attempts to bring over an English Company everyone who reads the 'United Irishman' will see the objects of his attack. Had he written a criticism no one would have minded, but he let his real feelings appear. First he says the acting was not incompetent and it was not bad, yet it was ineffective. My brother, in his professional days, toured every hole and corner of Ireland and has sat in their cottages with the people and knows them better than Mr. Martyn. Many people have recognised how lifelike was his performance.

"But as in the case of the Literary Theatre, when anyone tries to build up here, somebody else tries to throw down . . . The bitterness of what he has written will recoil on himself. I may tell you between ourselves that I suspect George Moore has helped to get Martyn to write this attack because I cannot believe that Martyn would do such a thing unaided. If he did, however, he ought to remember that we are of the people and that the movement in Ireland is of the people and that in the end we and not he will win."

Not that Martyn was in the least anti-national. He had confessed to George Moore that he would like to write his plays in Irish. He had written "Maeve" which Yeats saw as the symbol of "Ireland's choice between English materialism and her own natural idealism, as well as the choice of every individual soul." Although Martyn stood apart from the early struggle for existence of the Irish National Theatre Society and the Abbey Theatre he did not forget his theatrical interests and in 1914, when the Abbey was in one of its low periods, he helped to found "The Irish Theatre" as a revival of the Irish Literary Theatre and he no doubt knew that one of his colleagues, Thomas MacDonagh, offered the management of the company to W. G. Fay. This modest proposal to set up in competition with the Abbey was in the air as early as 1912 but never went beyond preliminary inquiries and a suggestion that W. G. Fay would be worth a salary of £150 a year.

After the "Deirdre" and "Kathleen ni Houlihan" show the Fays were hoping to persuade Alice Milligan to approve of their reviving "The Last Feast of the Fianna" and they feared that their chances might be spoiled by Martyn's attack on their ability as actors. The approach to Miss Milligan was left to Yeats but nothing came of it. Frank Fay then started after another quarry and wrote to Yeats:

"Mr. Russell has been telling my brother of a little comedy you had in your mind about a man who made soup out of a stone. Have you started writing it and will you let us try our hands at it?" He repeated his confidence in there being a good supply of plays but kept harping on the difficulty of the "hall" and shuddered at the idea of having to go to the Antient Concert Rooms again, "which is a horrid place and very expensive."

"I know what Wagner did and what Antoine has done, but they were both men of irresistible genius and nature had given them the fighting qualities that would enable them to do their work. Besides they lived in countries vastly different from Ireland where the majority are willing slaves. I find myself continually saying 'Oh that the Irish Literary Theatre had built a hall'!"

It was probably a very good thing that this did not happen, for although the Abbey Theatre was always physically inadequate for its company it was at least specially designed as a theatre. A "hall" built according to the half-formed ideas of Martyn, Moore, Yeats and the other luminaries of the Literary Theatre would have been as amorphous in design as the aims of its sponsors were amorphous.

But the birth of the Abbey Theatre was coming nearer. The group known as W. G. Fay's Irish National Dramatic Company was just about to merge into something bigger. "One of our people" Frank Fay wrote "suggested the formation of what he calls an Irish National Theatre Society, but he has not worked out his idea and personally as I said before I dislike asking for people's money. It is certain that one of these days Mr. Digges and Mr. Kelly will have to be paid if we want to retain them." This letter was in reply to one from Yeats dated April 21, 1902:

Dear Mr. Fay,

I have written a long reply to Edward Martyn in which I have renewed my praise of yours and your brother's company. I want to make people understand the importance of the St. Teresa's Hall experiment, and to prepare them for future work. You might join in if you see a chance. When Edward Martyn said to me that your brother over-acted his part I was not quite sure at first that there was not some truth in it. I was trying to find out the cause of the laughter, and as you know was planning alterations in the play, blaming myself in chief. Friday night convinced me, however, that none of the blame was your brother's and very little of it mine. I did not criticise the acting in my letter to you not because I hesitated to tell you what I thought but because I really did not feel competent. In two or three years I shall understand the subject, but I don't yet. I know that all the acting of verse that I have seen up to this has been wrong, and I can see that you and your brother have struck out a method which would be right for verse, but till I have seen that method applied by many different people, I will only be able to criticise acting very vaguely. George Moore has more precise ideas because he likes the 'natural school' and has therefore many examples to judge by. Two years ago I was in the same stage about scenery that I now am about acting. I knew the right principles but I did not know the right practice because I had never seen it. I have now however learnt a great deal from Gordon Craig.

"Now as to the future of the National Theatre Company. I read your letters to a wealthy friend who said something like this. 'Work on as best you can for a year, let us say, you should be able to persuade people during that time that you are some-thing of a dramatist and Mr. Fay should be able to have got a little practice for his company. At the year's end do what Wagner did and write a "letter to my Friends" asking for the capital to carry out your idea.' Now I could not get from this friend of mine whether he himself would give any large sum, but I imagine that he would do something. I think we must work in some such way, getting all the good plays we can from Cousins and Russell and anybody else, but carrying out our theories of the stage as rigorously as possible. The friend I have quoted is interested in me but Russell has his own following, and I think it likely that we will ultimately get a certain amount of money. I will do my best to do a great deal of strong dramatic work in the immediate future. I should not talk about what my friend said to me. It is all too vague, but I quote it to you to show how the wind may blow."

There is hardly any doubt, that although she was referred to as "he" the friend in question was Miss Horniman who was then acting as Yeats's secretary and amanuensis at Woburn Buildings in London. Fred Ryan was working away at his proposed constitution for the new society and this proved to be the year when the roots of the Abbey Theatre were really beginning to sink and spread.

Chapter Three

NATIONAL THEATRE

THE records of the early Abbey Theatre days would be much more complete but for the disappearance of a brown metal hat box. Like some graver matters this can be blamed upon the Black-and-Tans. The house we lived in, in Upper Mount Street, had a bad name at Dublin Castle and was often raided, usually in the middle of the night. The hat box attracted attention several times because it was difficult to open. After being bayoneted one night it was put away in the back of a coalhole to save further trouble. It was never seen again, nor were several hundred letters it contained, from Yeats, Lady Gregory, Synge, Miss Horniman and others to Frank and Willie Fay.

Fortunately quite a few letters did survive and Frank Fay was a great cutter out and paster in scrap books. So it is still possible to discover in some detail how the work of establishing the new group went on. The Fays gave up their part of the title and "Irish National Theatre Society" was chosen. No doubt the new name was a joint inspiration for in spite of an earlier reference to Fred Ryan's having suggested it Frank Fay said in 1908 in New York that he had invented it himself. This was when, so short a time after helping to create it, the Fays were being criticised or almost persecuted by Yeats and Lady Gregory because their American producer, Frohman, insisted on putting the I.N.T.S. title into his advertisements when the Fays and their small company were playing in New York just after they had left the Abbey.

Frank Fay told his New York audience that the Society wanted A.E. (George Russell) as president, who had given them their first Irish play. But A.E. suggested that Yeats would be a better choice so ". . . I proposed Mr. Yeats who was, and is still, president of the Irish National Theatre Society. The title, if I remember rightly was suggested by me because at that time I was greatly excited by an article which William Archer wrote in 'The Morning Leader' describing how Bull had formed the Norwegian National Theatre out of a handful of young men and women who had answered an advertisement inserted by him in a Bergen newspaper."

The original book of rules, which remained in force until after the Abbey Theatre was opened, stated that the objects of the Society were "to create an Irish National Theatre, to act and produce plays in Irish or English, written by Irish writers, or on Irish subjects; and such dramatic works of foreign authors as would tend to educate and interest the public of this country in the higher aspects of dramatic art." Most of the rules were of the sort which the Chief Registrar of Friendly Societies would understand, if nobody else. But there was one important exception; Rule VI established a "Reading Committee" of six who were to consider all plays proposed for performance by the Society. "No play shall be performed until it has been recommended by the Reading Committee. The final acceptance or rejection of any play shall rest with the Members of the Society, to whom such plays shall be read at meetings summoned for the purpose, when a three-quarters majority of those present shall decide. The author shall not be allowed to be present when a vote is taken."

A sub-section of this same rule said that no official could accept or reject plays on behalf of the society, and another that no play should be accepted or rejected "on political grounds solely", and the literary, dramatic and acting merits were to be primarily considered. No objection to a play "on the ground that its performance would antagonise any political party shall be valid unless it should be considered that there is any degradation of National ideals in the work submitted. The rights of the Stage Manager were laid down in Rule VII.

The signatories to this book of rules were to constitute the Society until a general meeting had been held to appoint a President and admit other members. There were seven of them,

the first official founders of the Irish National Theatre Society :
William G. Fay, Patrick J. Kelly, Frederick Ryan, Helen S.
Laird, Maire Walker, James Starkey and F. J. Fay with George
Roberts as Secretary.

The political rule no doubt seemed quite a routine matter
at the time, though it would never have occurred to the Fays
or to Yeats or to Lady Gregory to write it down. In 1910, it
became an awkward one to argue about, for Miss Horniman
threatened to withdraw her subsidy—and in the end did—
because she said the Abbey theatre had made political gestures
in breach of an agreement with her. She was a woman of the
utmost originality of mind and could therefore see political
significance where others might miss it. During the riotous
first performances of "The Playboy of the Western World" the
players were particularly incensed by Trinity College boys
singing "God Save the King". One or two of them hissed from
the stage: no doubt a most unprofessional thing to do. But this
is what Miss Horniman made of it in a letter to the directors,
dated February 1, 1907:

"I am informed by Mr. Hugh Lane that low behaviour (I
mean hissing) took place *from* the stage and that this hissing was
political. Now I am of course aware that everyone was in a great
state of excitement that night and maybe got carried away.
But it must be clearly understood that I will not allow my theatre
to be used for political purposes and the actors must be informed
that hissing the drunken vulgarity of the stalls is just as bad as
the patriotic vulgarity of the pit.

"I am fighting for us to stand above all low political spite on
either side. I make this protest at once, it is a matter of honour
that the directors should do their best to prevent conduct in the
actors which would justify my closing the theatre. From the very
first and ceaselessly I have held firm to the position that *I will
have no politics*. I should despise the idea of bowing low to the
Castle, you know that by my suggesting Kathleen for next week.
Yours sincerely, A. E. F. Horniman."

Nobody could have known or guessed, when the rules were
being drawn up, that any such significance would ever be given
to the word "political". Nor could anybody have been sufficiently
clairvoyant to know that the Society would prove so unstable.

Within a few years W. B. Yeats was the only one of the founder members left active in the national theatre (Lady Gregory was an early member, but not one of the first). The rest had left the Society in various quarrels, or had simply lost interest, or had emigrated.

When the Abbey Theatre came into being its business was taken over by a limited company, so the original I.N.T.S. rules were then replaced by those of the "National Theatre Society, Ltd.". In some ways the new rules went into even more detail by dealing with what should happen to the shares of members who proved to be illegitimate or who became insane or bankrupt. The powers of the stage manager disappeared and control was vested in the directors. The Reading Committee also disappeared. The looser rules were naturally an advantage since no theatre can be run as though it were a democracy. The I.N.T.S. was started by people with high ambitions and little experience. They had evidently gained in wisdom by the time they formed the N.T.S. Ltd.

The first founder members were soon joined by Dudley Digges, Thomas Koehler, J. H. Cousins, Frank Walker, Padraic Colum and Harry Norman and the secretaryship passed from George Roberts to Fred Ryan. W. B. Yeats was elected president ; Maud Gonne, George Russell and Douglas Hyde vice-presidents.

The choice of Yeats was a wise one for he was much more than an impressive figurehead. He was a would-be man of the theatre who quickly learned much of the craft, though he remained invincibly ignorant on some sides of it. Almost thirty years after leaving the Abbey Willie Fay still wrote of him (in 1935): "Mr. Yeats agreed to be our president, and hence, from the first production of the Irish Literary Theatre down to the present day he has been the head and guiding influence of the Irish Theatre." When inviting Yeats to be president Fred Ryan was able to say that a small hall had been rented for a year at less than £1 a week. It was a small warehouse, draughty, dark and cold. But it was the first home of the Irish National Theatre. Edward Kenny (in the "Irish Times") gave a good description of it making it clear that although the "Camden Street Room" was a failure as a theatre it made a successful headquarters. As a meeting place, he wrote, it was ideal ". . . and it was not long before literary Dublin found its way down the dark entrance passage. The place became the focal point of the whole theatre movement; all of the major developments of the Society's early years were discussed there, and a representative cross-section of the city's cultural life was always to be found there." Lower Camden Street was well out of the way for theatrical or literary people, but they had something to go for in those busy days. The little theatre in Camden Street was an important lodging place on the way to the Abbey Theatre: there is nothing left of it now but the walls, for it was burned out after a Black-and-Tan raid in 1920 having become a Republican meeting-place.

The original plan was to open the new "theatre" with Yeats's "The Hour Glass" and "A Pot of Broth" in December, 1902. "I want to alter the title of 'The Beggarman'." Yeats wrote in September "Please change it to 'A Pot of Broth' in any public announcement. I have a sufficient reason for this which I have not time to explain now . . . I think it would be a mistake to have verses for the opening of the Theatre. Such things are never done well and give the air of a penny reading entertainment . . . Hyde has done several new plays, including a most beautiful Nativity play, and will I think throw himself heartily into your work."

A few days later Frank Fay wrote again to say that "The Hour Glass" had been put aside because it was not thought possible to give it the preparation necessary for such an important piece. At the same time, in spite of Rule Six and the Reading Committee the brothers jointly turned down Lady Gregory's play "Twenty-five". Obviously they either relented or were over-ruled for the play was put on a few months later with W. G. Fay in the leading part.

The change of plans for the Camden Street opening meant bringing in Fred Ryan's Ibsenish comedy, "The Laying of the Foundations," a choice which was criticised because the play was regarded as too much under foreign influence. So for the first night the plays were, in addition to Ryan's "Foundations", "A Pot of Broth" by W. B. Yeats, "Eilís agus an bhean déirce" and (for one night only) "The Racing Lug" by James Cousins. It should have been a tingling, exciting occasion when the Irish National Theatre Society played for the first time in its own home

An Artist's impression of the ABBEY THEATRE before the fire

THE PIT ENTRANCE : Where theatre lovers entered

THE VESTIBULE : The scene of many brilliant gatherings

THE WOLF-HOUND DRAWING which has made history as the
coverpiece of the Abbey Theatre programme for many years

THE VESTIBULE AGAIN: Showing the scene of Sarah Purser's
portrait of Sarah Allgood

and presented two plays written specially for its company. But the audiences on December 4, 5 and 6, 1902 were small and apart from known devotees, not enthusiastic. The newspapers were cold and scornful. The "Evening Mail" wondered if it would not be possible "to house more honourably the much-advertised Irish Dramatic Muse". The critic complained that the scenery was poor, the stage too small, Fred Ryan's play "trivial" but at the same time "pungent". He saw much earnestness and "some very creditable acting, notably by Mr. F. J. Fay and Mr. Digges." He liked "A Pot of Broth" but did not stay for "Eilís agus an bhean déirce" (which was perhaps the first recorded instance of walking out on the play in Irish; a practice which has not ceased even now), and although there were only 50 in the audience, the last to arrive being George Moore, a number of them slipped out with the "Mail" man.

Bringing "The Racing Lug" into the programme on the Saturday night did not help much, but the "United Irishman" announced that the performances had been financially successful and expected crowded audiences in future now that the Society had been "fairly launched". To mark the fact that it was indeed launched and had the fullest support Yeats wrote an article in the October issue of Samhain to record the winding up of the Irish Literary Theatre which, he said, had been planned for only three years of life. He gave the short history of the I.N.T.S., sketched its methods and rounded off his notes for the year by rebuking Edward Martyn for arguing that the actors should try to train themselves for the modern drama of society. "Plays about drawing-rooms are written for the middle classes of great cities, for the classes who live in the drawing room, but if you would uplift the man of the roads you must write about the roads, or about the people of romance, or about great historical people." He made the inspired guess that if the company stuck to poetry and the countryman ". . . we may recover in the course of years a lost art which, being an imitation of nothing English, may bring our actors a secure fame and a sufficient livelihood."

Fame and livelihood were still far away and there was not much rest for the actors. They took their plays out to Rathmines for a Gaelic League concert where the advance publicity invited Irish Irelanders to "Come and see what the Irish National

D

Dramatic Company are doing to build up an Irish theatre. Irish plays—consequently wholesome. Plays by Irishmen for Irishmen and produced by Irishmen." There was a little touring, also, and the "Munster News and Limerick and Clare Advocate" noted that the players visited Foynes "through the kindness of Lord Monteagle."

It was quickly agreed that the Camden Street experiment was a failure and in spite of the advantages of a "theatre" of its own the I.N.T.S. decided to go back to playing in hired halls. One more play was produced there—"The Sleep of the King" by James Cousins, the last he wrote for the society. It was not long before he went off to take up a teaching post in Tokyo and Fred Ryan a job of writing anti-British propaganda in Cairo. But in spite of the disappointment about the hall in Camden Street a lot had been achieved and 1903 was to prove one of the most fruitful years—the year of Synge's arrival and of Sara Allgood's and the year of the first visit to London when the great critics of the big newspapers first began to notice that something worth while was happening in Dublin (they made this discovery well in advance of the Dublin critics). The planning of programmes was rather fluid. "The Hour Glass" which Yeats would have liked to see staged in the first programme was being rehearsed for the middle of January. In the end it was not put on until March (at the Molesworth Hall) and by that time a lot of work had already been put into preparing "The Shadowy Waters" for production in May. Willie Fay wrote to tell Yeats of this decision "At last night's meeting the crowd decided to play the 'Shadowy Waters' and Columb's play for the next show which we reckoned to give in the last week of May". Neither decision was carried out. Four other plays reached the stage before Padraic Colum's "Broken Soil" and "The Shadowy Waters" did not come until after that.

It is difficult to guess how the little company found time to do readings and rehearsals and detailed planning of a play which was postponed for more than a year and at the same time work on two new plays for the current production. But somehow they made the time by hard work and long hours. Frank Fay had a theory that a lot more progress could be made if people would do work at home. He asked Yeats to write down some detailed criticisms of the small-part players. Not, he said, that he and Digges or Kelly were above criticism—"but at least we work, so does Miss Walker. None of the others, so far as I can judge, trouble themselves to do anything between one rehearsal and another." Of course, this was applying professional standards to amateurs and Frank Fay became keener on the idea with every play he worked in but there were members of the Society who could not see the sense of such labour. They were in for the fun of it, as amateurs usually are, but the really lazy ones did not last long. It would hardly have occurred to them, as it did to Frank Fay, that there was any virtue in learning by heart "The Death of Cuchulain" to be used as a stopgap recitation in emergencies. He did this after taking fright at the fact that during "Eilís agus an bhean déirce" a performance had to be cancelled at the last moment because one of the girls did not turn up and no Irish-speaking understudy was available.

Both Fays were anxious to put on Yeats's "The Land of Heart's Desire" but here they ran into the same sort of uninstructed religious prejudice which had caused trouble with "The Countess Cathleen". Digges would not hear of doing the play and others agreed with him. Ryan, Cousins, Starkey, Koehler, Roberts and Miss Laird were willing but they were hardly a strong enough team. Frank Fay said he saw nothing wrong with the expression "tortured thing" used by the Faery Child to describe Christ on the cross—"and I think it would be a pity to remove it; but when the young blood of the Catholic University, who may be supposed to represent something of the progress Ireland has made, objected to the "Countess Cathleen" it is hardly likely they would swallow that 'insult' to their religion. The older folk would not and the Gaelic League is absolutely fossilized on the same question . . . The principal reason that has prevented us from doing the play has been a desire not to lose Digges. I am inclined to think that even though he did not play in it himself he would smell hell if he associated with us. . . Miss Walker once suggested to me that a holy picture might be substituted for the crucifix . . . but Digges thought we had better let such plays alone. Personally I would play a Freethinker or an anarchist or anything that would shock the Toryism of the Irish Catholic but it may not be judicious".

The religious difficulty was always somewhere around the corner in the early days of the national theatre. It required some courage occasionally to defy convention and present to an untrained and narrow-minded audience some play or passage which was unconventional or at any rate open to question. Most of the questions would be thought hardly worth asking by Irish Catholics today, for the change in attitude was already beginning and in only eight years it was perfectly feasible to put on "The Land of Heart's Desire".

The programme of the I.N.T.S. for Saturday, 14th March, 1903, at the Molesworth Hall was "The Hour Glass" and Lady Gregory's "Twenty-five" (against the Fays' judgment). In the interval Yeats gave an address on "The Reform of the Theatre" in which he was able to use some of the ideas put to him in Frank Fay's memoranda. There was nothing remarkable about the performances or about the lecture, but the audience was a good one. The "management" picked up one of the habits of the commercial theatre by presenting bouquets to the ladies at the end of the show, which Joseph Holloway—later the architect for the conversion of the Abbey and a careful archivist—thought most inappropriate. Some of the newspapers remained cool but "The Leader" and the "United Irishman" took the performance seriously and wrote about it respectfully. Yeats had used no manuscript for his address and told the readers of the "U.I." that since then he had also forgotten most of what he extemporised. The press reports and the few notes he sent to the "U.I." gave a fair notion of what he had told his audience. His first point was that plays had to be found or written which would make the theatre a place of "intellectual excitement"; his second that speech must be made even more important than gesture on the stage.

"I have no doubt of our being able to do this, for Mr. W. G. and Mr. F. Fay have already taught their principal actors better speaking than I have heard in any English theatre. Thirdly acting must be simplified, getting rid of everything restless that draws attention from the voice; and fourthly something would have to be done about scenery, to give the actor a fitting background."

The company was on the move a little in April, visiting
Loughrea and Galway with "Deirdre" and "A Pot of Broth".
"The Laying of the Foundations" was revived and put on
at the Rotunda for a concert. During this month, too, the Society
put out a pamphlet explaining its objects. When some argument
arose about this explanation Frank Fay said he had written the
pamphlet himself except for the opening sentences which he had
altered after discussion with Yeats. There were people then who
well knew that it was misleading to say that the I.N.T.S. had
"grown out of the movement which the Literary Theatre inaugurated," but the same sentence said that the society was
formed "to continue—if possible on a more permanent basis—
the work begun by the Irish Literary Theatre." That was perfectly true; the other fell a little short of perfect truth even though
it was apparently approved of by the Fays themselves. At the
time it was written, however, there could have been little doubt
in anybody's mind that what the I.N.T.S. had grown out of was
as much the Ormonde Dramatic Society enriched by the ladies
of Inghinidhe na hEireann as it was the Irish Literary Theatre,
impoverished by the lack of Irish actors.

The attitude of the Dublin press was on the point just now
of being altered. On May 1st, 1903, a telegram arrived for Frank
Fay from Stephen Gwynn giving him the name of an hotel in
South Kensington where rooms had been booked for members
of the society. Gwynn had seen the productions of "The Laying
of the Foundations", "A Pot of Broth" and "Eilís agus an bhean
déirce" and had been deeply impressed. He quickly got in touch
with Yeats and opened negotiations for a short visit of the players
to London where he was president of the Irish Literary Society.
The negotiations took some weeks and when they were finished
and the visit arranged Frank Fay warned Yeats to say nothing
in London which might lead his friends to expect anything out
of the ordinary. This was not false modesty. He dreaded London
because he thought the programme originally chosen was uncharacteristic. "Of course the peasant plays are a novelty" he
wrote to Yeats "but I should have preferred 'Deirdre' or
'The Hour Glass'. The latter two besides showing a special
kind of acting would show versatility. However the matter is
now decided but I do feel it is idle going so far to play O'Loskin."

O'Loskin was his part in Ryan's "Foundations". He had to play it in London, but by a last minute change "The Hour Glass" was included in the programme. There were to be two performances on one day, "The Hour Glass," "Twenty Five," and "Kathleen ni Houlihan" in the afternoon, "The Laying of the Foundations," "A Pot of Broth" and again "Kathleen ni Houlihan" in the evening. It was a big undertaking for these young men and women to travel from Dublin to London to put on their plays. They were nearly all at work of some kind and had to get a Saturday morning off. But somehow they managed it and sailed on Friday night, May 1st, to give London and Dublin a theatrical surprise and something to talk about for a long time.

Chapter Four

1903—ANNUS MIRABILIS

I N the London theatre nowadays a Saturday first night is not common; for one thing it is an irritant to the critics of the Sunday newspapers. But fifty years ago it was no rarity and on Saturday, May 2nd, 1903, there was an opening at the Avenue Theatre of George P. Bancroft's "The Little Countess". Most of the chief London critics, therefore, could see only the matinee performance by the Irish players. A high proportion of them were willing to trail out, well off their beat, to the Queen's Gate Hall in Kensington to watch the amateurs and A. B. Walkley enjoyed himself so well that, apart from what he said in the "Times" he wrote personally to Yeats saying he was vexed that a "stupid theatre elsewhere" prevented him from seeing the evening's plays. Barrie was in the audience, and Henry James, but Shaw missed the plays by two days and wrote saying he was sorry because he particularly wanted to see the new methods.

Frank Fay found it a strain waiting in the wings to go on as the Fool in "The Hour Glass" but he and the others were at the top of their form and the plays went without any hitch. The company had to rush off to their hotel for a quick dinner between performances and at this point one of the ladies announced, twenty minutes before the curtain was to rise, that she was too ill to go on. An understudy volunteered, Stephen Gwynn announced her name to the audience but this seemed to act as a tonic to the original actress who suddenly recovered and carried on with her part so that the second performance went as smoothly as the first. The chief burden of the experiment fell on Willie Fay who was responsible not only for the travelling of the company

55

and the stage management, but for playing three important parts in one day. The players slept well that night and set off back for Dublin on the Sunday morning, no doubt sharing the train to Holyhead with one of the many English travelling companies which visited Ireland in those days, and probably feeling for the first time something of the sensations of being professionals. Maire nic Shiubhlaigh's recollection was that they were "flushed from our victory and not a little awed by the high praise which had been showered upon us."

The London critics had not been quite unprepared for what they saw at the Queen's Gate Hall. Stephen Gwynn had already written of the I.N.T.S. company in the "Fortnightly Review" in an article called "An Uncommercial Theatre". Yeats's work was known in London, the poet himself was a familiar Bloomsbury and Fleet Street figure and a certain amount of his personal publicity (conducted with the help of Miss Horniman and others from Woburn Buildings) spilled over on to the Dublin players. There were even among the audience some Londoners who had already travelled over to Dublin to see what Mr. Yeats was up to.

But the English newspapers had not printed much about the acting and the Fay methods were known only by hearsay. In his memoirs Willie Fay recalled that there was "not a discordant voice in the full chorus of praise". This was a more sanguine view than the press notices justify. The "Daily Telegraph," for instance, coldly noted that the Society was ". . . apparently a collection of young literary enthusiasts who, with the ardour of youth, seem inclined to attach to their work considerably more importance than its quality warrants as yet" and the critic could discern nothing in the way of "a fresh development or a new departure either in 'stage-methods' or subject matter."

The "Morning Post" and the "Daily News" were kinder, though the "News" man (Philip Carr) thought that ". . . Much of it was crude, much of it uncertain even to the point of failure in its effect." But Carr saw the beginnings of a "peculiar and native convention in dramatic art." He also defined the meaning of a "national" theatre clearly—the subject being under discussion in London then, as it is over fifty years later and the British National Theatre no nearer being built.

"With these productions of the Irish theatre" Carr wrote "we feel that in Dublin the theatre is beginning to be what it has not been for hundreds of years in England—the expression of the aspirations, the emotions, the essential spirit and movement of the people, both in the sense in which it is so in France, in the sense of being a recognised platform to which come those who have something important to say and those who seek something important to hear, but also in the sense in which it expresses the idealism and poetry of the national sentiment." Carr's interest in the Irish company persisted and a few years later he was responsible for its first visit to Paris.

William Archer in the "Manchester Guardian" was calmly objective, praising the acting a good deal and concluding that the performances amply justified what had been heard of the Irish National Theatre. He wrote at greater length in "The World" a few days later without repeating himself, but with more reservations. Among the individual performers he thought "Mr. W. G. Fay showed extraordinary accomplishment in his part of the Beggarman in 'A Pot of Broth'. This was a perfect piece of acting—perfect no less in its sobriety than in its humour. In two other parts played by this Mr. Fay he was clever but a little nervous and inaudible. . ." The "St. James's Gazette" was sharply sarcastic in its notice written by "the unregenerate ordinary dramatic critic, who has been unable so far to discover any reason for apprehending that the Thames will be set on fire by these pleasant but in no way remarkable amateur theatricals. But no doubt we shall know better some day." The "Pall Mall Gazette" and the "Westminster Gazette" were kinder and the "Star" harped on the absence of "national" drama in England: "There seems perhaps a touch of coxcomby in the announcement of a company of amateurs whose appointments we could probably have bought up with the spare cash in our pockets as an Irish National Theatre. But consider what their claim to such a title implies—that a dozen unimportant people, acting a parochial drama and a drama of the soil with such talent as they have gathered from their surroundings do to some extent dramatically represent Ireland to a greater extent than any fashionable drama

being acted today within our sacred halfmile radius of Charing
Cross can possibly be said to represent England."

The greatest success among the notices was the "Times"
whose critic, Walkley, decided to hold over his opinions for
a Friday Literary Supplement where he had room to expand.
There was hardly a word in the long notice which was not praise,
though Walkley noted "a touch of affectation" in the acting,
something of the self-importance of children dressed up for
a grand domestic occasion. But he turned this into a virtue—
"All new movements in art" he concluded "are selfconscious,
abound in little exaggerations and affectations. Is there not an
Irish precept, 'be aisy; and if you can't be aisy, be as aisy as ye
can'?". Walkley found the "Irish gentlemen and ladies" good
to look at: "The men are lithe, graceful, bright-eyed, and one at
least of the maidens, with the stage name of Maire Nic Shiubhlaigh,
is of a strange, wan, 'disquieting' beauty . . . As a rule they stand
stockstill. The speaker of the moment is the only one who is
allowed a little gesture . . . When they do move it is without
premeditation, at hap-hazard, even with a little natural clumsi-
ness, as of people who are not conscious of being stared at in
public." Walkley approved of the scenery "of Elizabethan
simplicity", realised the musical possibilities of English when
spoken by Irishmen who were not burlesquing and bathed his
mind in the restful, resigned, sad mood of the plays.

Another good notice came from E. K. Chambers in "The
Academy & Literature". It contained an error of fact which
Yeats was quick to correct. He wrote to the Editor: "Your
sympathetic notice of our Irish plays and players has it that
they were produced under my direction. They were produced
under the direction of Mr. W. Fay our stage-manager, and Mr.
F. Fay our teacher of speech, and by the committee of our
dramatic society. Mr. W. Fay is the founder of the society,
and from the outset he and I were so agreed about first principles
that no written or spoken word of mine is likely to have influenced
him much. I on the other hand, have learned much from him
and from his brother, who knows more than any man I have
ever known about the history of speech upon the stage."

When the players returned to Dublin, or rather when the
London papers followed them, the hard work of the last few

years seemed entirely justified. Not all the English critics had been kind, but all had been attentive, their judgment unclouded by any national prejudice except that in favour of the "stage Irishman" and their editors had been liberal with the space. It was a turning point. The Dublin newspapers and the Dublin gossips were struck by uncertainty and hesitancy. Might there not, after all, be something in these players in spite of the fact that they were Dublin "boys and girls"?

Could the London critics have been so interested in a society which was doing nothing more than "amateur dramatics"?. It was noticed that, although no such claim was made on the programme, most of the London papers referred to the group as the Irish National Theatre. Word seemed to get quickly around the newspaper offices that the Society had better be looked at more carefully. Press notices became longer, some even became more respectful. But the extreme nationalists were not to be won over by praise from English lackeys of imperialism. They became more suspicions than ever, and suspicion soon broke out into hostility. And just around the corner was a man on whom their hostility could be vented successfully—John Millington Synge.

How quickly the trouble began after the reading in June of "In the Shadow of the Glen" can be guessed from a passage towards the end of this letter from Yeats to Frank Fay, dated August 8.

". . . I am sending your brother Seanchan today. (If you are reading it, pronounce 'Shanahan'). If I can get them done I shall send at the same time the maps of the more important positions. I think it will play about an hour and a half. It is quite a long elaborate play, and is constructed rather like a Greek play. I think it the best thing I have ever done and with the beautiful costumes that are being made for it, it should make something of a stir. I am afraid you will have an exhausting part in Seanchan but you will find plenty to act and the best dramatic verse I have written to speak. Your brother told me he meant to cast you as Seanchan, and I am very glad of it. I have long wanted to see you with some part which would give you the highest opportunities. Your playing of the Fool in the Hour Glass was beautiful, wise and subtle, but such a part can never express anyone's whole nature. It has to be created more or less from without. Your performance of Seanchan will, I believe, establish all our fames." He mentions then some measurements for a curtain which he regards as most important because it was to be the background for ". . . a prologue spoken by Mr. Russell in the Wise Man's dress." This never happened. Whatever the reason, Yeats explained it in the first edition of the play as ". . . owing to the smallness of the company nobody could be spared to speak it."

"Russell hears" he ends "that there were 'brilliant rows' last Monday, but he doesn't know what they were about. I suppose there is no secret; if not I should like to know. All theatrical companies make rows but ours seems to have more than the usual gift that way."

The reply, which no doubt let Yeats into the secret, is missing but I think I can guess what it contained. Strange as it may seem now "In the Shadow of the Glen," the purest piece of story-telling, was thought offensive and even insulting to Irish dignity. On all hands there were attempts to have the production stopped and the refusal to withdraw it, backed by the Fays and Yeats, caused the loss of one of the best young actors, Dudley Digges. He left the society with several others, including Maire Quinn (who was later to be his wife) and felt so strongly about the play that he went to the first night with Maud Gonne and staged a demonstrative walking out of the theatre. Digges went to the United States not long after and he became the first of the Fay-trained Irish players to make a mark first on the American stage and then in Hollywood. Valuable as he was his loss was a small thing compared with the acquisition of Synge. Yeats was 37 at the time and Synge six years younger. Synge died at 37, Yeats at 73. If they had both lived, which would have been the greater dramatist in the end? An unanswerable question. Shaw lived 40 years longer than Shakespeare, but lost the advantage by writing himself out twenty years before he died. So it would be rash to say that beyond doubt Synge would have developed greatly, but there is nothing rash about saying that it would have been amazing if he had not. There were many contrasts between the two men. Yeats had been a sensitive emotional child who got little benefit from school and did not go to university at all. Synge had the bustling childhood of one in a large family.

He went to Trinity College, was a musician of almost professional standard (Yeats, on Miss Horniman's authority, was tone deaf) and he travelled a lot. By the time Yeats met him in Paris in 1898 Synge was a practised writer and journalist. He had a private income which for those days was substantial—something between four and five hundred pounds a year, so his living in poor surroundings in Montmartre or the Latin Quarter was a matter of preference rather than necessity.

When he returned to Ireland to write plays he went about it with such vigour and nervous energy that although writing them was not easy for him, they needed little alteration once he was satisfied with the text. He worked at the early drafts as though they were demons to be fought with and was not exaggerating when he said that writing "The Well of the Saints" was agony and horror to him. Synge expressed his human side much more than Yeats did in letters. He mentions his health a good deal, apologises for his hot temper, gently criticises his colleagues, but always with a touch of humour. He wrote to Frank Fay in March 1904: "It was very good of you to come out to look for me last Saturday and I was very sorry indeed not to have been able to see you. I was in bed with an abscess on my face—at the root of an old tooth—which without being in any way serious made it impossible for me to talk and disturbed me so completely that you would not have known me. It came on after the show on Thursday evening—I'd had a toothache all that day and I suppose got a chill in some way. I regret endlessly to have had to miss the two other performances as there were many things I wanted to consider with a view to London . . . I do not know at all how long it will be before I can go to town again in the evening. I have been up again today and yesterday but I am very weak as I had high fever and the abscess isn't quite gone."

His concern with his health was not an exaggerated one for he was not strong. In fact in the year before he died when he was to have an operation, he sent Yeats a hurried note in pencil which he said was to be delivered only if "anything should go wrong with me under the operation or after it". He was worrying about his papers, said there was a certain amount worth preserving including the first and third acts of "Deirdre of the

Sorrows" and a lot of articles about Kerry and Wicklow that might be made up into a book; (it was the "Manchester Guardian" which had encouraged Synge to make a specialty of Irish travel articles and some of them were illustrated by Jack Yeats). There was also a lot of dross, or so he thought it, which Synge did not want to have reprinted. He asked Yeats to consult with others about selection. "It is rather a hard thing to ask you" he ended, "but I do not want my good things destroyed, or my bad things printed rashly—especially a morbid thing about a mad fiddler in Paris which I hate. Do what you can. Good luck, J. M. Synge."

His ending was typical—that he should be wishing Yeats good luck when he needed it so much more himself. It showed the warm, tender man behind the rather severe outside appearance. It displayed the quiet gentleness which covered the steel, sharp and highly tempered, in the character of John Millington Synge.

For the moment Yeats thought affairs were going smoothly enough although, according to Hone's biography, it was about this time that he seemed uncertain whether his dream-theatre would be realised in Dublin. He can hardly have guessed how near it really was to realisation. The "designer" he referred to in his letter about the "Hour Glass" was staying at Coole Park with Lady Gregory. She was Miss Horniman who had long been an ally of Yeats's in his occult activities. She was now showing a practical interest in his plays and he too was prepared to concentrate his efforts. He had been busy in London with John Masefield, Gordon Bottomley and others working on an idea for a poetic theatre. Yeats was one of "the Masquers" who were planning to produce "plays, masques, ballets and ceremonies" in London with Arthur Symons, Gilbert Murray, Sturge Moore and Edith Craig on the committee. Nothing much ever came of the project.

Meanwhile some competition was being felt in Dublin from a rival society which was more interested in propaganda than the Fays or Yeats were. The poet was not disturbed, though he thought Digges might go over to the opposition, "I think that a political theatre would help us greatly in the end" he wrote to Frank Fay in September 1903 ". . . by making it easier for us to keep a pure artistic ideal. It will satisfy the propagandist feeling and at the same time make plain the great effectiveness of our work. . . . I think we should all welcome this new theatre in every way we can and keep it from causing bad feeling. Much later, this rival organisation, which was first named the Theatre of Ireland and then, merging with another organisation, The Irish Theatre was to cause a lot of bad feeling but it certainly seemed no danger at all in 1903 and was even useful in convincing Miss Horniman that the I.N.T.S. could safely be regarded by her as non-political for she was determined at all costs to keep out of "wicked politics".

The new season opened on 8th October, 1903, at the Molesworth Hall, Dublin, with the two new plays "The King's Threshold" and "In the Shadow of the Glen" and a revival of "Kathleen ni Houlihan" in which Sara Allgood appeared for the first time with the company, though not yet as a leading actress. She and her sister who used the stage name of Maire O'Neill were to prove by far the outstanding creators of the "Abbey tradition" among actresses. Two Dublin newspapers thought the performances worth greeting with leading articles. The "Evening Telegraph's" was friendly, though it criticised Yeats's technique as a dramatist. The "Irish Daily Independent and Nation" was anything but friendly and spoke of the Society's aims being "perverted" by Yeats. The inspiration of this attack was doubtless an article in the "United Irishman" which had got hold of a copy of Synge's play ("by treachery or carelessness," Willie Fay thought) and had smeared it in advance as ". . . a crude version, pretending to be Irish, of the famous or infamous story about the Widow of Ephesus."

The morning papers had conflicting accounts of the reception given to Synge's first play. The "Daily Express" judged from the demeanour of the audience that the piece was generally understood to have some polemical significance, some underlying moral idea, but happily "this was not so obvious as to force itself into notice without previous specific warning". The critic was not, apparently, a reader of the "United Irishman", otherwise he would have had warning specific enough. Jack Yeats contributed an article which showed that the "United Irishman" was, whatever its prejudice, open to contradictory views. He also provided a sword to Synge's enemies by greeting the comedy

as an attack on "our Irish institution, the loveless marriage".
"All are relieved when at the end of the scene the young wife
goes away with a young tramp, who tempts her by his life on the
open highway and under the open sky—better be a young
tramp's drudge, better be a target for everyone's scorn, better
anything than the foulness of such a marriage . . . Thus is the
lesson enforced . . . that morality will often gain its ends by
loosening the ligatures."

The "Irish Times" man wrote: "This production, which has
led to a secession, or schism, in the Society, was received with
mingled cheers and hisses. Personally we think that the morality
which could be injured by witnessing it must have been so
excessively weak-kneed to start with as to be quite unworthy
of consideration." But the play was found, in the end, to be
"excessively distasteful" and Synge was advised to find some
other way of occupying his "distinct power, both in irony and in
dialogue" than by using it for "casting slurs on Irish womanhood," a phrase which seemed to have slipped in from some much
more naive or even native publication.

The "Freeman's Journal" thought differently, calling the
play "a quaint Irish comedy, depicting in colours true to nature
an episode in the lives of a man and woman living in a lonely
home in one of the glens of Wicklow." It observed that at the
end of the piece "Mr. Synge was called before the curtain and
received a most flattering ovation." The "Evening Mail" which
had prodded the Society once or twice before found no offence
in the play and was glad to see the idealism of propaganda being
leavened with realism. The "Independent" showed a less liberal
spirit than the "United Irishman". Having attacked Synge
before seeing his play it hit just as hard afterwards. The only
virtue its critic found in "In the Shadow of the Glen" was brevity.
Otherwise its characters were unreal, its tone unhealthy and
"from first to last it is nothing more or less than a farcical libel
on the character of the Irish peasant woman." A writer in the
"Leader" found it "for its length . . . one of the nastiest little
plays I have ever seen." "Figaro and Irish Gentlewoman" came
to the rescue by saying "The play was certainly not untrue
to life, and shows much ability; but it was not a pleasant one,
though full of humour". And "Irish Truth" was jubilant because

Synge had asserted the right of the educated man "to look at life as it is, even amongst the idyllic hills of holy Ireland, where in spite of clerical shackles Nature still asserts her claim over the material which crawls between earth and heaven."

Nothing could be more welcome, from the purely realistic point of view than such a chorus of dissonance and contradiction. It was all publicity even if some of it was harmful (the anticlerical note in the support of "Irish Truth" for instance). This sudden increase of Irish newspapers' interest, combined with long reviews from the London critics, brought much larger audiences than usual and it was worth while reviving the performance for one night later in the month. "The King's Threshold" which Frank Fay had forecast was to make "all our fames" was not exactly overlooked in all the fuss about Synge but it hardly made the expected impact. Wiser and more experienced management would have separated the two plays. The conflict of ideas on what Synge was trying to do and what the National Theatre ought to aim at was summed up in two letters in the "United Irishman" from James Connolly and Maud Gonne (who was by this time Mrs. MacBride). Connolly advised Yeats to think again about the functions of a National Theatre but encouraged him to ignore the "yelpings of the 'Independent' and the babbling voices of the Philistines and iconoclasts." Maud Gonne said that the national theatre must appeal to the masses (which by any decent Marxian standards belonged to Connolly's world) ". . . and if the Irish people do not understand or care for an Irish play, I should feel very doubtful of its right to rank as national literature, though all the critics in England were loud in its praise and though I myself might see beauty in it." Having now withdrawn from the Society she did not hesitate to drop hints which might easily have been about Miss Horniman. "Mr. Yeats asks for freedom for the Theatre" she ended her letter "freedom even from patriotic captivity. I would ask for freedom for it from one thing more deadly than all else—freedom from the insidious and destructive tyranny of foreign influence."

The profitable and prophetic hurly-burly about Synge went on almost until the next programme was ready for production on December 3rd, 1903. "The Hour Glass" was revived with Frank Fay instead of Digges as the Wise Man and George

E

Roberts as the Fool. In "A Pot of Broth" Maire ni Gharbhaigh (who later became Mrs. George Roberts) replaced Maire Quinn and thus it was proved, in one of the earliest of the great Irish theatrical quarrels that nobody was indispensable or irreplaceable. George Roberts was one of the most enthusiastic of the pioneers, first as an actor, later as secretary to the Society and, perhaps most valuable of all, when a partner in the firm of Maunsel & Roberts as publisher-in-ordinary to the Abbey Theatre. He was a fiery redheaded man, nimble-tongued and never at loss for a word in conversation, or most of all in argument, at which typically Irish pursuit, he was frighteningly proficient. Long after he had left Dublin I used to meet him in London, in Fleet Street, where although white-headed and no longer very quick on his feet he was as articulate as ever and full of stories about Yeats and Synge. In "The Hour Glass" he had one of his best parts, but it was not the chief play of the evening. This was a three act play by an author who, still not having made up his mind about a nom de guerre, called himself Padraic MacCormac Colm. It had taken more than a year to put together, for Colum had been working on it for some time when he wrote to Yeats in December, 1902, saying "I have left the Fiddler play over since I read it to you. But I have re-constructed the whole thing. The plot is quite simple now, I have cut out all the literary matter and am going to avoid the 'literary picturesque'. It will be in three very short acts. I commenced the second act today. . ." He wrote from the Irish Railway Clearing House and signed himself P. J. Collumb. The audience were enthusiastic, the press a little less so. The "United Irishman" sneered at Colum's immature inadequacy but the critic who signed himself "Spealadoir" was contradicted the following week by Oliver Gogarty, who found much virtue in the young poet's work.

This group of plays was the last activity of 1903, which Willie Fay called the *annus mirabilis* of the Irish National Theatre Society. It was the year which brought Miss Horniman, John Millington Synge and Sara Allgood into the Irish National Theatre. It was also the year which took Maud Gonne, Arthur Griffith and several of the regular actors out of the Society. The successful visit to London had commanded a little more respect from the Dublin newspapers which were not keen on

Mr. Yeats or his works and pomps but it had also given a new opening to the nationalists who could criticise on a new ground —that the Society was being misled by English praise. "In the Shadow of the Glen" had given the National Theatre its first taste of public vituperation. It had not shared in the troubles caused by "The Countess Cathleen" and since then the mob-censors had been silent (they have hardly been heard of since "The Plough and the Stars" and that was in the 'twenties).

Synge's arrival contained the seed of much greater events, but the one of most immediate importance was Miss Horniman's growing interest in Yeats's writing for the theatre. She had already financed him in London when "The Land of Heart's Desire" was put on, with Shaw's "Arms and the Man" at the Avenue Theatre. She had frequently helped Yeats's occult friends with generous sums of money and when a curator of the Horniman Museum, a family foundation, lost his job Miss Horniman, convinced that he was a victim of injustice, paid him for some time a pension of £8 a week out of her own pocket. She was a rich women by the standards of 1903 and the Dublin players had already benefited from her wealth for she had found the money for the expensive mounting of "The King's Threshold" as well as herself designing and making the costumes and she immediately promised to pay for the costumes of "The Shadowy Waters" which was to be the first production of 1904. At this time Yeats commented coolly on her "King's Threshold" designs: "Miss Horniman has to learn her work however and must have freedom to experiment. I think her 'Baile's Strand' will prove much better. I have told her the old sages permitted elaborated dress though not elaborate scenes and this combined with the fact of its being a court misled her into overdoing colour and the like in certain parts."

But Miss Horniman was well content. On the second night of "The King's Threshold" she had written to Yeats ". . . do you realise that you have now given me the right to call myself artist? How I thank you."

She was a woman of quite amazing strength of character, but judged from her correspondence not always likeable. When she needed a telegraphic address she remembered that Shaw

had once called her an octopus and so chose the word "Tinten-
fisch"—the ink fish that spurts out a black cloud when pursued.
The good she did by subsidising the Irish National Theatre
Society and providing it with the Abbey Theatre is a debt which
Ireland never had any chance of repaying. The harm she did
by her letters to Yeats after the Abbey was launched has never
yet been fully realised or assessed. St. John Ervine said that
she ". . . did more to raise the quality of the English theatre
than any other person of her time." He hardly exaggerated for
apart from what she had done before coming to Dublin (one
must take it that Ervine meant more precisely "English-speaking
theatre") she left in her final huff to found the Gaiety Theatre
in Manchester which certainly enriched the British theatre with
dramatists and actors. Even the biographical chapter in Rex
Pogson's "Miss Horniman and The Gaiety Theatre" can put
forward no convincing reason why "a middle-aged, middle
class, suburban, dissenting spinster" (which is her own description)
should show such a passion for the art of the theatre that she
should found the first subsidised playhouse in any English speaking
country and after that put into the Manchester theatre years
of work and of unearned income which the citizens of Manchester
never seemed to appreciate. At least they stayed away from her
Gaiety in such numbers that in the end she had to close down and
sell out to what she called a "movie man". But John Masefield
would have none of the theory that Miss Horniman's money and
effort had been wasted. "Looking at it now" he wrote to her
"you must see that it has been a glorious success, for all over
England, in towns and villages, the theatre is springing up with
quite new wonderful life . . . It may not be the end any expected,
but it is a living consequence of your first establishing the theatre
here."
    Those consequences were beyond any forecasting however
as Miss Horniman, on Yeats's suggestion, began to study in
Joyce's history of Ancient Ireland so that she might understand
the problems of designing for "On Baile's Strand". He left her
to this work while he went off on a lecture tour in the United
States during which he first began to scent the possibility of
massive support for the Irish Theatre from the Greater Ireland
across the Seas. While he was on the spot he inquired into an

invitation for the Society to visit St. Louis for an exhibition which was to be held there. He wrote from 1 W. 87th St., New York City on December 30:

My dear Fay,

It is very hard to find out the truth about the St. Louis project. Since writing to you I have got an opinion which is quite the reverse of Thomas's. Major McCrystal, who is a prominent Gaelic League propagandist here, thinks that our theatre would be a success in St. Louis. All I can say under the circumstances is that it would be well for you and your brother to suspend your judgment until you hear further from me. I will send you all the information I can so that you will form your opinion with fairly full knowledge before you. I am going to talk the matter over with Byrne, whose judgment in a matter of that kind would be excellent, and next Monday I go to St. Louis itself and will write you as soon as I can after getting there.

"Miss Horniman has sent me some notices of the plays and I have seen the other papers. I know pretty well now how they have been received. I think that the reception of the plays has been the best we have yet had. I do not say this because it is more enthusiastic than the reception of our plays before, but I notice that we are now accepted as a matter of course as an established institution. I am inclined to think that the coldness of the United Irishman towards us is helping us in several quarters."

Yeats discovered two people in the United States who were on the point of starting to write books on the "intellectual movement" in Ireland one of whom he thought might write something important and influential. He was content with his success after doing twenty out of a programme of forty lectures, having met the President, Theodore Roosevelt (". . . found him extraordinarily well informed about our whole movement—indeed, one of the best read men I have met.") and been given a reception by the New York Press Club. He said he always felt that the success of the Irish plays in London had been discounted because of natural Irish suspicion of English opinion, but American opinion, he reasoned, could not be discounted and if it turned out possible to get the company to the United States, Yeats thought that would be the greatest gain of all. He seemed to have been thinking about the reception of "The Hour Glass" and guessed that ". . . it will be criticized more favourably a little time hence. My impression from the performance I saw in Dublin and from the performance I saw in London was that it held the audience throughout but that their afterthoughts were sometimes a little hostile. Some of them felt that because I had written it, it must of necessity contain some hidden heresy, while others, finding it impossible to believe that I really thought those things, supposed I had written it out of mere archaistic emotion and that it was therefore a mere literary experiment. I hope you will try and put off the performance of Baile's Strand as long as you can, as I may not be able to be back by the 20th of February. I may be kept here a week or two later. My trip to the coast will take over twenty days and I find that I am getting new engagements here. For example I have just heard that I am going to be invited to give four lectures in the Catholic University of Washington. I wish I could have seen you in the 'Hour Glass'. Judging by what I have heard your 'Wise Man' was a beautiful performance. Please tell Colm how delighted I am at his success and please set him to work on a new play if you can."

"On Baile's Strand," although in active preparation was not to be produced until the end of 1904 when it was the first play to be seen on the stage of the Abbey Theatre. However, Yeats still treated it as imminent and wrote a long letter about it in January, 1904, which is given in full in Allan Wade's "The Letters of W. B. Yeats." It enclosed some new dialogue and explained how epic and folk literature can ignore time as drama cannot—"Helen never ages, Cuchullain never ages." But as a dramatist he said he had to recognise the passage of time because Cuchullain ". . . has a son who is old enough to fight him." It is this letter which contains the mild criticism of Miss Horniman's work as a designer. But she was capable of criticism too, and not always mild. A fragment of an undated letter, of about this time, criticises Yeats for tone-deafness, unknown persons for rudeness to him and accuses some speakers (possibly Frank or both Fays) of trying to do something beyond their abilities. ". . . Mr. Yeats cannot hear *tones,* think it polite not to make him aware of the facts of the case. Personally I consider that he is being treated as a blind man would be if he were insulted by ugly faces being pulled at him by people who spoke politely to him all the while. Quarter tones are such extremely delicate things that no amateur is to be trusted with them except in very rare cases. If you do anything with notes, do them 'purely'; or else leave them alone altogether and trust to the ordinary speaking voice and its various degrees of tones. There is nothing in this letter which is not simple musical fact and I wish that you would shew it to any friend who can play any instrument or sing. With kind regards, Yours sincerely, A. E. F. Horniman."

It was just as well that the two friends were aware of certain shortcomings, however small, in each other for they were about to join in an enterprise which quickly demanded from them a lot more tolerance than Miss Horniman found it natural to employ and a greater patience and humility than came easily to Yeats.

Chapter Five

LONDON AND DUBLIN

IN the middle of January the I.N.T.S. put on its first production
of 1904. There were two new plays "The Shadowy Waters"
and Seumas MacManus's "The Townland of Tamney" with
a revival of "Twenty Five". The "Irish Times" found the Yeats
play "quite unsuitable for staging" and perhaps there was a
touch of uncertainty about the fact that it was described on the
programme as "a dramatic poem." The audiences and some
of the critics found difficulty in understanding what somebody
in the stalls called Yeats's "unintelligible mysticism" but they
must have been surprised and even made uneasy when they read
what Tom Kettle had to say in "New Ireland". "Surely" he
wrote "to anyone who believes at all in the existence of the soul
there never was a play so actually translucent?" He was inspired
to continue with some thoughts on the future of the National
Theatre and his summing-up was "We want a National Drama
that will believe in life, in this actual, concrete, everyday life
that flows about us and slides ever through our hands. The present
generation is pre-eminently an economic generation in Ireland,
and we want playwrights who will see the poetry of it." He also
thought it would be a good thing if people would stop identifying
the National Theatre too exclusively with the works of W. B. Yeats.

Almost as if it were a reply to this the Society chose for its
next programme in February a play by A.E. and one by Synge.
"Deirdre" and "Riders to the Sea" gave the critics more to
argue about than today's playgoers could ever imagine. In
his "Irish Literature and Drama" (1936) Stephen Gwynn
described "Riders to the Sea" as ". . . a brief masterpiece whose
quality has never been challenged, even in Ireland" and the

play inspired C. E. Montague to one of his most piercing passages of description in "Dramatic Values". But Gwynn must have forgotten the first production. The "Irish Times" which seemed to be running out of words to express itself again said "unfit for presentation on the stage". What the critic had to say occupied ten lines, a pattern in its way, of how to greet a masterpiece: "Of Mr. J. M. Synge's play 'Riders to the Sea' it is difficult to say exactly what one thinks. The idea underlying the work is good enough; but the treatment of it is to our mind repulsive. Indeed, the play develops into something like a wake. The long exposure of the dead body before an audience may be realistic, but it certainly is not artistic. There are some things which are lifelike, and yet are quite unfit for presentation on the stage, and we think that 'Riders to the Sea' is one of them." This stung a reader "F. T. C." to write a second notice in the form of a letter to the Editor in which he gave an outline of the play and named the players. Under the signature "The writer of the notice" the critic replied, quoting seven lines of Coleridge and twenty-four of "Hamlet" and devoting a dozen lines to "Riders to the Sea". He did, however, finish by saying ". . . I wish well to Mr. Synge and to the Irish National Theatre, and should be very sorry knowingly to say one word that would be hurtful or unfair to him or any of his fellow-workers". The "Freeman's Journal" found the play "mournful almost to weirdness" but said that on the second night it had "considerably advanced in the appreciation of the audience." Other compliments paid to Synge were that his introduction of a corpse on to the stage was "the cheap trick of the Transpontine dramatists." In the "New Leader" the critic called "Chanel" thought A.E.'s play beautiful but unreal and Synge's "hideous in its realism. . . . the most ghastly production I have ever seen on a stage." But "Chanel" thought there was hope for Mr. Synge. "If he can learn to avoid the morbid, and to take a saner and less crabbed view of existence, I think he may be capable of writing a really valuable play, a play which, while it is healthy, shall yet be effective. If we could arrive at a man between Synge and A.E. we would have the ideal."

A week after the production Synge wrote from 31 Crosthwaite Park, Kingstown : "I regret endlessly to have had to miss the two other performances as there were many things I wanted to consider with a view to London. It can't be helped and it is well I saw one. What do you think of 'Chanel'? I do not know at all how long it will be before I can go to town again in the evening. I have been up again today and yesterday but I am very weak as I had high fever and the abscess isn't quite gone. I will go in as soon as I can safely."

"With a view to London" meant that another trip organised by the Irish Literary Society was being planned. There were to be five plays at the Royalty Theatre on Saturday, March 26th, 1904—"The King's Threshold," "The Pot of Broth," "In the Shadow of the Glen," "Riders to the Sea," and Colum's "Broken Soil." It was the first time the players had ever been on a real stage in a real theatre with the grandeur of the occasion emphasised by the fact that interval music was provided by the Pearl Assurance Orchestra. In the audience were Mr. Wyndham, the Tory Secretary of State for Ireland, Sir Henry Campbell-Bannerman, leader of the opposition, Lord Aberdeen, Lord Lieutenant of Ireland, Mrs. Humphry Ward, Bernard Shaw, J. M. Barrie, and (although not noted by any of the gossip writers) James Connolly. Yeats was there, back from the United States, where his trip had been financially profitable and good for the prospects of the Society whenever it chose to cross the Atlantic.

This time the volume of the press notices was greater and there was generally more praise. A few critics, including C. E. Montague and Max Beerbohm, spotted "Riders to the Sea" for what it really was; the "Daily Telegraph" was less cool, the "Morning Post" even more warm. There was a hint of political trouble; perhaps because of Wyndham, Campbell-Bannerman and Aberdeen (the very personification of British rule) being in the audience, the young London-Irish were more than usually demonstrative. At any rate William Archer in "The World" was angry with Yeats for saying in a curtain speech (he was harder to keep behind a curtain than most dramatists) that it was easy "to know when we have our own people in the house." Archer said that the English were no less enthusiastic and why should Yeats be in such a hurry to diminish his great poetic success into a party demonstration?

Walkley, in the "Times Literary Supplement" thought the applause sometimes sounded like a parti-pris demonstration. He also thought Yeats altogether too cock-ahoop and much preferred Willie Fay's "modest and stammered thanks". In fact considering his more than friendly greeting for the first visit, his second notice might almost be called carping. He had the insight to open with a warning that the chief danger to the Society was premature success or becoming fashionable. He even detected a "demi-semi-calculation" in some of the accents which had seemed so natural before. H. W. Nevinson, in "The Speaker" found another meaning for Yeats's remark about "our people". It was only the poet's modest and polite way of saying that the applause of the house might have been more kindly than deserved. There may have been a touch of irony to this but Nevinson was no man for half measures in praise. He described Padraic Colum as "the youngest of the Irish poets who are now leading the only intellectual movement in these islands that counts". His dogged interpretation of "The King's Threshold" in terms of Liberalism and Toryism was a little tiresome, but for novel interpretation of an Irish play J. T. Grein took the prize with the unique comment that "In the Shadow of the Glen" was "something a la George Bernard Shaw with an Ibsenish touch for final note."

The Irish papers left the visit to be dealt with in short paragraphs by their London correspondents but the weeklies had special articles. One in the "United Irishman" by "D. O'D." was so unfriendly that James Connolly wrote a reply putting the critic, whom he presumed to be a woman, in her place. His retort included a piercing analysis of "Riders to the Sea" —almost up to the C. E. Montague standard. The argument went on into June and never reached any conclusion, though the reader might deduce that Connolly had more feeling for the theatre than "D. O'D.".

Synge was obviously excited by the London visit. He stayed on after the company had gone home and from 4 Handel Street wrote to Frank Fay: "Many thanks for your letter. We have indeed had a great success with our show and a good deal of our criticism has been most interesting although I still believe —as I once said to you—that our real critics must come from

Dublin. It is only where an art is native, I think, that all its distinctions, all its slight gradations, are fully understood. For instance most of our recent London critics have spoken well of the two plays we gave them that were perfectly obvious—I mean 'Riders to the Sea' and the 'Pot of Broth,' but most of them failed to grasp 'Seanchan' ['The King's Threshold'] and the 'Shadow of the Glen' both of which demand an intellectual effort to make them comprehensible or at least a repeated hearing. However that may be we have so far *no critics* in Dublin so we have to make the best of London. I do not think Archer wrote the notice in the "Manchester Guardian." At least they say at the Irish Lit. Soc. that the Guardian sent a man down specially from Manchester to do our shows, and further the opening paragraph of the notice seems to imply that the writer had not seen our company before. Whoever he may have been he seemed to understand the theatre—he was the only critic I think who put his finger on the faults in the writing of 'Broken Soil'. Have you seen Max Beerbohm in *yesterday's* Saturday Review? What he says of dramatists' technique is excellent, much more sensible it seems to me, than Archer's sort of snub at our short plays in the "World". Still Max B. writes some amazing folly—as you will see—as where he says Irishmen cannot be vulgar. I wish he could see "Sold" [by J. H. Cousins, revived at the Queen's Theatre, Dublin in 1907]. Archer seems to criticise—at least our prose plays—as dramas first and literature afterwards. The whole interest of our movement is that our little plays try to be literature first—*i.e.,* to be personal, sincere and beautiful—and drama afterwards. I dare say Archer admires Sudermann!

"To come nearer home. Frankly I think our Irish audience are a little to be excused for staying away—that is rather an Irish way of expressing it. With Seanchan we drew good houses, but 'Broken Soil' is not strong enough as the main piece of an evening. 'Shadowy Waters' is still less so and Deirdre is weak also.

"I am not blaming our choice of plays, we gave the best we had, but I think we should not take a gloomy view of our audiences because they did not let themselves be persuaded that weak plays were strong. When we have a bigger and better repertoire

—that is the matter of life and death—we will draw better audiences. I do not much believe in trying to entice people in by a sort of political atmosphere that has nothing to do with our dramatic movement. By all means have '98 plays—I will do one if I can—but *strong* and good dramas only will bring us people who are interested in the drama, and they are, after all, the people we must have. I think the verdict of the London Gaels that 'In the Shadow of the Glen' is perfectly unobjectionable will make the Dublin writers a little afraid of making themselves ridiculous by attacking us again on the moral question.

"I don't know that I can give you any criticism on the acting that would be of value. You should try and get more people— though I suppose that is not easy. The soldier [Thomas Koehler] and the Monk [Fred Ryan] in Seanchan were dreadful—the soldier especially. You are perfectly right that it is practice the crowd needs most—*i.e.*, of course practice of plays in public. Camden Street work is all very well but it will never take them beyond a certain pitch. Again all our women are too young; where else will you see such girls holding an audience—as they did after all—in serious drama? It was worst in the Shadow of the Glen. Miss W. [alker] is clever and charming in the part, but your brother is so strong he dominates the play—unconsciously and inevitably—and of course the woman should dominate. You were admirable I think in both your parts.

"I am very well but in agony and horror over my play with the blind people. It is exceedingly difficult to make it work out. I will be back in Ireland in 3 weeks about and hope to see you all then before I go off for my summer wandering. I fear I have written incoherently, I am tired, excuse it, very sincerely, J. M. Synge. P.S. please remember me to everyone."

That is the longest letter of Synge's that I have found but it seemed worth printing in full as showing his close interest in the detailed work of the Society, an interest which was more practical and more intense after he became a director. His idea of writing a '98 play came to nothing though perhaps it was in search of ideas for it that he went to the Queen's Theatre a year or two later to see one of the Irish melodramas that were played there at the time. It was "The Shaughraun" with Jimmy O'Brien (a favourite comedian for many years in Dublin) playing Conn.

Synge was sufficiently impressed with what he saw to write down some impressions of it for "The Academy". "It is unfortunate" he remarked "for Dion Boucicault's fame that the absurdity of his plots and pathos has gradually driven people of taste away from his plays." He found that some of the characters "had a breadth of naive humour that is now rare on the stage. Mr. James O'Brien, especially, in the part of Conn, put a genial richness in his voice that it would be useless to expect from the less guttural vocal capacity of French and English comedians, and in listening to him one felt how much the modern stage has lost in substituting impersonal wit for personal humour." A dozen years later Sean O'Casey was visiting the same theatre, seeing the same plays, or the same sort of plays, and learning the same lessons. I think he has said somewhere that his ambition when it was first fired was to write a play good enough for the Queen's and that he had not the Abbey in mind at all. Impressed as he was, there is not the slightest sign that Synge allowed his play-writing technique to be affected by the older methods of Boucicault, though he was never too haughty to borrow a plot or a theme (nor is any great dramatist, for that matter). Some of the London critics were reminded of Heyerman's "The Good Hope" when they saw "Riders to the Sea"; Arthur Griffith thought "In the Shadow of the Glen" based on the tale of the widow of Ephesus. "The Well of the Saints" was traced by the scholars to Andrieu de la Vigne's "Moralité de l'aveugle et la boiteaux" and further still back, through de la Vigne's work to an anonymous 15th century religious play "Mystiere de Saint Martin". Synge is supposed to have told Colum and Yeats that "The Well of the Saints" was based on a pre-Molière farce the name of which he had forgotten. Neither of these plays had the stroke of inspiration which made the Douls, Martin and Mary, having had their sight saved wish to lose it again after a quick look at the world about them. But a Philadelphia scholar, R. K. Alspach of the University of Pennsylvania has suggested that this twist of the plot came from Patrick Kennedy's "The Blind Nun" which appeared in 1871 in his "Bardic Stories of Ireland". If the story had been written for him beforehand perhaps Synge would not have found that it was "exceedingly difficult to make it work out". Perhaps, being a man of independent and original mind, he even made the story up for himself, though such conduct, if it became general among writers, would leave the scholars little to write about to the " Times Literary Supplement."

The trip to London and Synge's growing grasp of his craft were not the only excitements of April, 1904, however. This was the month when Miss Horniman made her official offer to buy the hall of the Mechanics' Institute, Abbey Street, and a building next door, in Marlborough Street, and turn them into a small theatre. Her letter and the reply to it (both quoted in full in Lennox Robinson's "Ireland's Abbey Theatre") are the birth certificate of the Abbey. The acceptance of Miss Horniman's offer is dated 11th May, 1904 and it was signed by all the founder-members except P. J. Kelly, and all the original committee members except Dudley Digges and J. H. Cousins.

It is everybody's favourite story that the Abbey Theatre was built on the premises of the City Morgue: it sounds well when gloomy plays are being discussed. But although it is true that part of the building had been a morgue there are much more striking things about its history. In the first place it had been a theatre under several different names before Miss Horniman took it over; secondly the buildings had a place in the beginnings of the Fenian movement as headquarters in Dublin of the Brotherhood of St. Patrick. In 1830 the Abbey Street property housed the Theatre Royal which lasted nine years before being burned down and was used for a miscellany of theatrical entertainments, but not for "straight" plays because Dublin, like London, had its system of theatre monopolies and the rights of another Theatre Royal, in Hawkins Street, were not to be infringed. The building was restored after the fire and after a short stretch under the titles of Princess's Theatre and New Princess Theatre of Varieties and People's Music Hall it became, as if somebody were clairvoyant, The National Theatre, and was still using that name three years before Miss Horniman bought it. One of the partners in management of the National was a Mrs. Glenville which is no doubt the explanation of the surprising entry in "Who's Who in the Theatre" saying that the mother of Shaun Glenville the veteran comedian "was the manageress of the Abbey Theatre, Dublin". Two things killed this theatre: first of all a rival house, the Queen's turned common informer and the Chief Crown Solicitor suggested that the National had better cease being a "house of drama" so it became a music-hall again. Then the Dublin Corporation made such demands for new emergency exits (there had been a disastrous theatre fire in England a little before) that nobody thought it worth while spending money on the alterations. The theatre, under its penultimate title of Hibernian Theatre of Varieties, remained empty though it was sometimes used for concerts by the Mechanics' Institute which was the principal tenant of the property.

Around the corner in Marlborough Street there was no such theatrical tradition. In 1834 the building was the Dublin Savings Bank, in 1840 it was for six years the office of a General Emigration Agent (one of those who shipped Irish men and women like cattle to England, the United States and Australia).

Sutton & Co., had the property for a couple of years and it was in 1863 that the National Brotherhood of St. Patrick came on the scene. P. J. Stephenson in the "Dublin Historical Record" tells how the brotherhood was one of the recruiting grounds for early Fenians and was so described by John Devoy in his "Recollections". The Brotherhood was an open, not a secret society, and its weekly meetings were devoted entirely to oratory though accusations were made that the members secretly drilled with wooden rifles. One of the chief orators was John C. Hoey who wrote the American Civil War ballad, "That Damned Green Flag Again" which records the ubiquitous qualities of the Irish Brigade fighting on the Union side. After the Brotherhood left, the building was taken over by the Dublin Total Abstinence Society in whose Coffee Palaces the Fays were to do their first public performances twenty-five years later.

To these two buildings, 27 Lower Abbey Street and 2 Marlborough Street, Miss Horniman took the architect Joseph Holloway and asked him what could be done about making a theatre in them. Willie Fay went along too, so that the practical questions of stage space and electric wiring would not be overlooked. Holloway's estimate was that a theatre could be made, to conform with the Corporation's safety regulations, for £1,300. The properties were available on 99 years lease for £170 a year.

A quick decision was needed and Miss Horniman decided that she could afford the capital cost, mainly because some of her shares (in the Hudson's Bay Company) had suddenly shot up in value. Orders were given and the work put in hand on the understanding that although the theatre would remain Miss Horniman's own property the Irish National Theatre Society could have the use of it, free, whenever they wanted it.

The critics immediately found one thing wrong with the proposition. Miss Horniman made a curiously restrictive condition—"The prices of the seats" she said "can be raised, of course, but not lowered, neither by the Irish National Theatre nor by anyone who will hire the Hall. This is to prevent cheap entertainments from being given, which would lower the letting value of the Hall." Arthur Griffith thought it undemocratic and even unpatriotic. In acknowledging the generosity of the gift the "United Irishman" recalled that as "The Mechanics" the hall had its place in nationalist history and had resounded to the voices of Mitchel, Meagher and Smith O'Brien. Irish questions had been debated there, Irish concerts held, a patriot's body lay in state there when it had been refused admission to the pro-Cathedral. (This referred to Terence Bellew McManus, a Fenian, and to Archbishop Cullen who refused the pro-Cathedral for a lying-in-state). And here was an Englishwoman proposing that the artisans of Dublin should be kept out because there were to be no sixpenny seats. It was some years before Miss Horniman's restriction could be cast off and the pit seats offered at 6d. each for matinees, which enabled Winifred Letts to write her poem "For Sixpence" of which the last stanza was

> Sixpence the passport to this splendid world
>   Enchanted, sad or gay.
> And you the playboy of them all I saw
>   For sixpence—William Fay.

The mechanical problems were tough ones, but there was also a complicated legal position to be cleared up. As the National Theatre the hall had been closed by an appeal to the principle of theatre monopolies. If Miss Horniman's investment was to be guarded it was therefore necessary to find a gap in the monopoly

F

and fit the new theatre into it. This could only be done by applying to the Lord Lieutenant for a Patent, his control over theatre buildings being like that of the Lord Chamberlain in London though he had no powers of censorship.

The application was first heard on August 4th, 1904, in the Council Chamber of Dublin Castle by the Solicitor-General for Ireland, Mr. J. H. Campbell, K.C. A second application was listed for the licensing of a theatre in the Pavilion Gardens, Kingstown. Both applications were opposed on behalf of the Gaiety, the Royal and the Queen's theatres. Mr. Herbert Wilson appeared for Miss Horniman, saying that her object was "to establish and keep a well-regulated theatre within the City of Dublin and therein to perform all interludes, tragedies, comedies, preludes, operas, burlettas, plays etc." He described her as a lady of independent means, of well-known family in England. She had an absorbing interest, he said, in the development of Irish dramatic art, and he floated off on a cloud of rose-coloured recollection by adding that the "Irish Literary Theatre Society" had achieved great success and that "many of its plays were enthusiastically received both in this country and England". Miss Horniman, having the advantage of knowing about these successes of the Irish Literary Theatre "took a deep interest in their work, and being blessed with an abundance of this world's goods, concluded that one of the best ways in which she could utilise her wealth would be to assist in developing the society in its new form, and so to help the work of promoting Irish Literary Drama and the National instinct as regards drama generally". This was laid on with a trowel, for as soon became apparent Miss Horniman was not at all devoted to drama as a form of Irish national expression.

There was the usual sort of buffoonery among the legal gentlemen, as when Sir Horace Plunkett said that he thought the establishment of the proposed theatre would tend in its own way to promote the country's interests. Mr. Denis Henry, K.C. (for the Gaiety Theatre) then put the witty question: "What, even though there is no bar?" and got his laugh. The Solicitor-General suggested that counsel for the opposing theatres ought to get together and consider what form of patent would carry out the legitimate aims of the petitioners without threatening the established theatres. Mr. O'Shaughnessy said he had not thought about it from that point of view, so the hearing was adjourned so that the lawyers could put their wigs together and agree on a form of patent which was not to exceed six years in the first instance.

Before the second hearing the "Irish Times" in a leading article commented on the prospects of the Irish National Theatre Society. It said that their proposal to set up a permanent theatre deserved support, it recalled some of the severe things said about the Irish Literary Theatre and offered some advice to the new national theatre—assuming for this purpose that there was no doubt about the Patent being granted. ". . . We would like to give the members of the Society a few words of advice. They ought not to obtrude plays in Irish, they ought not to favour works written by members, they ought not try to be too austere or too exclusive." If these were sins then the national theatre was determined from the beginning to commit them as quickly as possible. The "Manchester Guardian," too, anticipated the Solicitor-General's finding by publishing a leading article which began: "It is good news for England that the Irish National Theatre has found the much-needed endower and is likely soon to have its own playhouse in Dublin . . . Now if all goes well it should justify the hopes that Mr. Walkley and other good judges have of it as the force most likely to help our own ailing stage back to health."

The hearing at Dublin Castle reopened after an adjournment of two days and the lawyers said they had reached a formula which would permit the national theatre to open without being a threat to the profits of the others. As the new theatre was being planned to hold fewer than 500 people and the Royal had 2,300 seats, the Gaiety 1,800 and the Queen's 1,300 it was never a very convincing argument that they could be threatened but competition was vigorous in the Edwardian theatre and the dog in the manger might have been described as the special domestic pet of theatre managers. The terms of the patent were that it should allow only "plays in the Irish or English language, written by Irish writers on Irish subjects and selected by the Irish National Theatre Society under the provision of rule 7 of the Society's rules." Otherwise the new theatre should be used only for concerts and lectures. The difficulty of Miss Horniman's being resident outside the country could be got over by vesting the patent in Lady Gregory. On Saturday, August 20th, in the Library, Dublin Castle, the Solicitor-General gave his judgment granting the patent on the agreed terms. He found no proof to support suggestions made in cross-examination at the first hearing that the Society had been responsible for productions of ". . . a somewhat immoral, anti-religious and highly political character." But in case anybody should go against his advice and attempt to run the theatre on such lines he reminded them that the patent was for six years only and that the Society was "on trial". The patent would cease if the society were dissolved, the theatre could not be enlarged, no licensed bar would be allowed. On these terms he advised the Lord Lieutenant to grant the patent to Lady Gregory in trust for the Society.

The "Evening Telegraph" trustingly concluded that "in the hands of the present conductors, Lady Gregory, Mr. Yeats and Dr. Douglas Hyde, the theatre can scarcely be expected to become a hotbed of political agitation. With the old legends predominating in the subjects, with the prominence that literary expression will receive, the fear is that the theatre may be somewhat too classical to be a popular or national force."

Chapter Six

A HOME AT LAST

AFTER the patent had been granted the work on the theatre was redoubled. Men from Millar & Beatty were busily measuring and fitting carpets; T. J. Sheehan was doing the electrical work, James Bill putting in the seats, J. & C. McGloughlin making the fireproof curtains and the metal porches for outside, Sarah Purser working at the stained glass and R. & E. Farmer pushing on with general constructional work. I wonder how many of these firms and individual craftsmen have left behind their records of fifty-odd years ago? Their letter files and ledgers would provide some footnotes to the history of the Abbey Theatre. They would certainly show up dramatically the contrast between the original cost of the Abbey and the price that may be paid for replacing it on an enlarged site—work which has been under consideration now since 1951. The original £1,300 will seem pitifully small compared with the hundreds of thousands required to put up the large new Abbey which is now believed to be necessary.

While the Abbey was being built Yeats and Frank Fay were preparing an onslaught on George Moore to demolish some argument of his about the staging of Ibsen's "Ghosts". William Archer had been brought in to clinch a point of argument but his reply seemed based on misapprehension. "By the way" he wrote in a postscript to Yeats "I hope if the I.N.T. should do any more of Ibsen's plays it will use my *revised* translations (one volume to each play) which are a great improvement on the old green edition." The letter was devoted entirely to "Ghosts" which was not at that time produced and never has been by an

Abbey company. Yeats's letter (26th August, 1904) commenting on Archer's shows a growing self-confidence in discussing theatrical affairs.

He wrote from Coole Park. My Dear Fay: I send you Archer's letter. You will see by it that you can't make very much out of that point in stage management. You can of course say that as Ibsen who always gave the stage directions when he was certain, did not direct the actor to stand up, the management is free. I rather suggest however that you go very little into details of this kind, for your audience will be interested in general principles they will not care three straws about Moore's competence. If I were you I would make your article an attack on realistic stage management. The position of attack is far stronger than the position of defence. Put Moore on the defensive and you will win. Be just to Antoine's genius, but show the defects of his movement. Art is art because it is not nature, and he tried to make it nature. A realist, he cared nothing for poetry which is founded on convention. He despised it and did something to drive it from the stage. He broke up convention, we have to re-create it. It would be quite easy for us to get a superficial finish by choosing for our stage manager somebody who understood the perfected though temporary art of Antoine and his school. To do this would be to become barren.

"We must grope our way towards a new yet ancient perfection. We can learn from nobody to recreate tradition and convention except from those who have preserved it. We have learned with devout humility from the players of Phèdre, and though our problem is not quite theirs it is like theirs, but unlike Antoine's. We desire an extravagant, if you will unreal, rhetorical romantic art, allied in literature to the art on the one hand of Racine and the other hand of Cervantes. . . There is the stage management that came to its perfection with Antoine. It is the art of a theatre which knows nothing of style, which knows nothing of magnificent words, nothing of the music of speech. Racine and Shakespeare wrote for a little stage where very little could be done with movement, but they were as we know careful to get a great range of expression out of the voice. Our art like theirs, without despising movement, must restore the voice to its importance for all our playwrights, Synge just as much as myself, get their finest effects out of style, out of the expressiveness of speech itself . . . Your brother understands, for instance, that in the first act of The Well of the Saints there must be long quiet periods, a suggestion of dreams, of indolence. The same is true of Kathleen ni Houlihan. Moore wanted Kathleen to walk up and down all the time in front of the footlights. When I explained that this would not be true to the play, that she was as it were wandering in a dream, made restless as it were by the coming rebellion, but with no more fixed intention than a dreamer has, he wanted me to re-write the play. . . .

". . . we have founded our own theatre because we and certain people who agree with us dislike [the commercial theatre]. The little fame we have won has come to us because we have had the courage to do this. You may as well keep this letter, as I have taken some trouble to collect my ideas and express them clearly. Lady Gregory, I know has sent you Kincora; the chief amendment is in the part of King Brian. It is now I think a very fine part, perfectly coherent, and with great dignity. At first Gormleith seemed to run away with the play, but now the balance is struck even. Yours sincerely W. B. Yeats.

"The Well of the Saints" and "Kincora" were not to be staged until February and March of the next year, but the Society was keeping up its original resolution to plan new productions well in advance. In fact, at a time when there must have been some wild exciting nights of hard work and talk, the young theatre was going on its way more surely. Yeats was thinking a lot about first principles and in "Samhain" he expressed himself more clearly than in his letter to Frank Fay which has some wandering passages though it makes a good point about Antoine and the Théâtre Libre. The Fays had never seen Antoine's company in Paris and what they learned at second hand made the Théâtre Libre an inspiration to them not because of its production methods (or "stage management" as the term then was) but because of Antoine's success in making a theatre out of nothing but amateur enthusiasm. Frank Fay had read himself into Antoine's mind but never took from it any principles of production. Antoine's attitude to the Parisian theatre of his day, which was in even more of a rut than the London theatre, also appealed to the Fays and to Yeats. But the mistake is made sometimes of thinking that the Abbey Theatre grew from a society which was trying to do the same thing in Dublin that Antoine had done in Paris. Their objects, national and artistic, were quite different, and their spirit was of a different world—though it has often been said that there is a type of volatile and spirited Irishman who is more at home in France than in England or, if he has any tendency to iconoclasm, in his own country. What the Irish theatre picked up from Antoine was not an artistic approach but a vital lesson in organisation.

Miss Horniman had made it clear that her own hopes for the new theatre were based on the dramatists rather than on the actors. She told Yeats that it was an article of his in the 1903 "Samhain," and his lecture on the Reform of the Theatre in the same year that decided her to make her generous gift. In a restatement of these principles Yeats said that the plays of the Irish theatre would have to be written "in the spirit of literature". He had a theory that the modern theatre was dying away because writers had thought of their audiences instead of their subjects. Nobody would ever accuse Yeats of thinking first about his audiences—at least not about his audiences in the theatre. "Method of production" came second among the fundamentals of the new theatre as he saw them. "If we are to make a drama of energy, of extravagance, of fantasy, of musical and noble speech" he believed "we shall need an appropriate stage management. He reviewed the history of stage management on the English stage, using Frank Fay's memoranda of 1901 and 1902; he boiled his opinion of Antoine down into three sentences: "An Irish critic has told us to study the stage management of Antoine, but that is like telling a good Catholic to take his theology from Luther. Antoine, who described poetry as a way of saying nothing, has perfected naturalistic acting and carried the spirit of science into the theatre. Were we to study his methods we might, indeed, have a far more perfect art than our own, a far more mature art, but it is better to fumble our way like children."

He touched on acting methods too: "An actor must so understand how to discriminate cadence from cadence and so cherish the musical lineaments of verse or prose that he delights the ear with a continually varied music. This one has to say over and over again, but one does not mean that his speaking should be a monotonous chant. Those who have heard Mr. Frank Fay speaking verse will understand me. That speech of his, so masculine and so musical, could only sound monotonous to an ear that was deaf to poetic rhythm, and one should never, as do London managers, stage a poetical drama according to the desire of those who are deaf to poetical rhythm." On the point of monotony there seemed to be a disagreement between Yeats and his father, J. B. Yeats who admired Miss Darragh for her wonderful "transitions" in voice and gesture and wished that the others "notably Frank Fay" had the same gift.

The last of Yeats's "first principles" was stage setting, a subject which had been neglected, on the whole, until Miss Horniman came along to try her hand at design. Yeats was unimpressed by an idea of Adolphe Appia, the Swiss designer then working in Paris, who had suggested that a man might be shown wandering through a wood by throwing the shadows of green boughs on him. But Yeats could not accept it. "I cannot persuade myself" he wrote "that the movement of life is flowing that way, for life moves by a throbbing as of a pulse, by reaction and action. The hour of convention and decoration is coming again." He also mentioned that Gordon Craig had done wonderful things with lighting. ". . . his streams of coloured direct light, beautiful as they are, will always seem, apart from certain exceptional moments, a new externality. One should rather desire for all but exceptional moments, an even, shadowless light like that of noon, and it may be that a light reflected out of mirrors will give us what we need."

Yeats was always fascinated by lighting, but very little was ever done at the Abbey to satisfy his ambitions. The first lighting was designed by Willie Fay and installed under his supervision. It was perfectly simple standard stage lighting as used in almost every theatre at the time, the only difference between one house and another being the intensity of light available: there were, of course, no movable spotlights for following players around the stage because (apart from their being nowhere to mount them) they would have offended against the very foundations of Abbey acting. In the 'twenties, after the theatre received its State subsidy for the first time some new lighting fittings imported from Germany were put in the front of the house on unsightly metal brackets; later some new dimmers were bought. Otherwise there was no substantial difference between the original lighting of 1904 and that which was destroyed in the fire of 1951. There never was a cyclorama or anything like it. Even a decent back-cloth was difficult because the stage was so shallow that players wanting to cross from one side to the other either had to walk out along the alley beside the theatre, or edge their way between the back wall and the backcloth: this was very much frowned on, when the curtain was up, and I can remember getting a severe reprimand for doing it from Shaun Barlow, the chief stage-hand, carpenter and general practical man.

It is perfectly clear that at this time Yeats believed it was the dramatists who were creating the theatre. Lady Gregory, ten years later, recollected it differently. "It is the existence of the Theatre that has created play-writing among us" she said and supported her assertion by giving the names of Boyle, Colum, Fitzmaurice, Murray and Robinson among the men who had turned to writing plays only after seeing the work of either the I.N.T.S. or the Abbey Theatre. In November, while "On Baile's Strand" was in rehearsal for the opening night ("the best play I have written" according to Yeats) and indignation was growing on the sixpenny seat issue there came the first setback of the fast-moving months. Although Miss Horniman thought the delay was to suit Lady Gregory's convenience it was the usual trouble of theatres that caused a postponement of the opening. It can very often be "all right on the night" if it is only that the actors do not know their words, the costumes have not arrived or, even if the author is still finishing the last act. But it cannot be all right if the theatre itself is not finished and Yeats was compelled in the end to announce the fact that there would have to be a postponement because the stage would not be ready in time to allow sufficient dress rehearsal. The delay no doubt worried him a little: Not so a hint from George Moore that he would like to be back in the swim. "I should have thought everybody knew by this time" he wrote from Woburn Buildings "that Moore's return to the theatre is out of the question. If there were not other reasons, and there are very sufficient ones, it is enough that he represents a rival tradition of the stage and would upset your brother's plans at every turn. He is very jealous of the success of the theatre and has been laying pipe to get into it for months past. He made up with me the other day. I also had my object (keep it to yourself) I want to get Dermot & Grania into my hands and think I see my way to an arrangement which will leave him free to do what he likes with it in England for a certain time; I to reshape it for you—it would make a fine verse play. . ."

In spite of the delay the cost of alterations and equipment for the Mechanics' Hall and the building round the corner did not much exceed Holloway's estimate of £1,300. Even allowing generously for the value of the gold sovereign compared with the pound note this was a modest amount. Irving's last production at the Lyceum ("Dante" in 1903) cost him £12,000 and he was not the only investor: perhaps the fact that the Lyceum soon went into liquidation suggests that this was a bit out of the way, but it was still an achievement in Dublin to build a decent little theatre for a tenth of what it cost to mount a single West End production. Even before the building was ready for handing over Miss Horniman was giving a direct subsidy. She needed somebody to watch on her behalf the progress of the building work and to make day-to-day decisions. Willie Fay was her choice and she offered him thirty shillings a week to give up his job as an electrician and become the first full-time member of the Abbey Theatre staff. This, like the cost of the theatre itself, was modest enough, for although the modern concept of the "film star's salary" was unheard of, and presumably undreamed of, there were leading players and music-hall top-of-the-bill acts which could earn £150 or £200 a week.

After all the last minute flurries had died down the Abbey Theatre opened its doors, calmly enough, on December 27th, 1904, a Tuesday. Lady Gregory was not there, but Miss Horniman was and so were Yeats, Synge, Russell and Martyn. The "Irish Times" described the audience as "fairly representative of literary and artistic culture" and the occasion as "an experiment, and possibly as an epoch maker, invested with unique interest." The "Evening Mail" was amused by the fact that the National Theatre, having started in a barn in a street named after an English viceroy, was now presenting Kathleen ni Houlihan

who ". . . purrs poetic sedition in a theatre granted for the
purpose by an Englishwoman; and she purrs it to an audience
of which no small percentage yield allegiance to that undis-
covered country which is known to the Irish Irelander as West
Britain." Yeats, naturally, made a speech, saying how indebted
the Abbey was to Miss Horniman for the home she had given
and for the freedom which went with it. One result of the small
costs was that the Society would be able to ask, before putting
a play on, "does it please *us?*" and not, until after this was
answered, the more usual question "Does it please you?". "We
will be able to be courageous, and can take as our mottoes those
written over the three gates of the City of Love by Edmund
Spenser—over the first gate was 'Be Bold', over the second 'Be
Bold for Evermore' and over the third 'Yet be not too Bold'."
The last was a good one for future use.

The "Manchester Guardian" sent John Marsfield over as
a special correspondent to describe the theatre and the first
performances. In spite of later improvements his description
was still an accurate one for many years afterwards and he
noticed that very special attention had been paid to the decoration. ". . . done by Irish people in nearly every case, under
the general management of Miss Horniman, though one or two
articles such as the carven figures of the electroliers came from
the Continent. On either side of the main entrance and in the
green-room are stained-glass windows designed by Miss Sarah
Purser, with the image of a tree in leaf. The entrance hall is
hung with a few portraits by Mr. J. B. Yeats, including a portrait
of Miss Horniman, the donor of the theatre and portraits of
Miss Walker, the "leading lady" and of some of the principal
actors. . . . It had been the wish of Mr. Yeats to have a projecting
stage, in the manner of the Elizabethan theatre, but it was found
that the projection in such a small building would occupy too
much space."

The readers of the "Manchester Guardian" at any rate were
not left in any doubt about Miss Horniman's part. That there
could have been no Abbey Theatre without her generosity
was hardly emphasised in the Irish newspapers though they
nearly all thanked her for the use of the hall. The "Irish Daily
Independent and Nation" got through a whole column on the

opening performance without mentioning her at all except as costume designer. This coldness persisted, inside. and outside the theatre among people who were against her on "national" grounds. She was an Englishwoman, intruding at a time when chauvinism was growing. She was also a rich woman among poor people, using her wealth to do what she believed was good. That assured her always of having a plentiful circle of enemies. She also had to face the rivalry of Lady Gregory, a jealous rivalry in which Miss Horniman in Dublin lost ground as fast as she had gained it in London when she had Yeats to herself so much during the secretarial sessions at Woburn Mansions.

Miss Horniman seemed to be trying hard at this time to make the best of her appearance, which was striking enough without any special adornment. A gossip writer described her as tall and dark, ". . . an interesting and artistic figure in a rich robe of crimson clasped with a buckle, on which is enamelled a cluster of peacock's feathers." Neither she nor Lady Gregory was a beauty compared with some of the young actresses—Maire nic Shiubhlaigh or the Allgood sisters for example—but Miss Horniman had a soft, compassionate and sometimes ethereal look (at least to the eye of the painter or the lens of the camera) which Yeats must have sometimes found more encouraging than the firm-lipped, heavy-browed stern stare of Lady Gregory. For the time being the rivalry between the ladies had no serious effect. Both had too much to think about and Miss Horniman was new enough to Ireland to be still patient though it must have been hard sometimes for her not to say "does anybody realise that *I* built this theatre?"

The more immediate trouble brewing was about Synge's new play "The Well of the Saints" which was to be the second new play at the Abbey. The usual sort of arguments started as soon as the rehearsals got going—the arguments that went on as long as Synge lived and that were a plague in O'Casey's day, among them the insistent voice of the actor or actress who did not like the lines and wanted them changed. A few small changes were made. The words "Almighty God" were cut in one or two places, though left in others. But there were stubborn complaints about Timmy's line ". . . And she after going by with her head turned the way you'd see a priest going where there'd be a drunken man in the side ditch talking with a girl."

Synge wrote about this in February, 1905.

Dear Mr. Fay, I have just come home from a long day in the country and found your letter waiting for me. Miss G. mentioned the matter of the speech about the priest to me directly but I had not time to go into the matter fully with her and see what she meant. In your letter you quote your objector as saying 'these things are not true'. What put the simile into my head was a scene I saw not long ago in Galway where I saw a young man behaving most indecently to a girl on the roadside while two priests sat nearby on a seat looking out to sea and not pretending to see what was going on. The girl of course was perfectly well able to take care of herself and stoned the unfortunate man half a mile into Galway. The way the two priests sat stolidly looking out to sea with this screaming row going on at their elbows tickled my fancy and seemed to me rather typical of many attitudes of the Irish church party. Further though it is true I am sorry to say that priests do beat their *parishioners,* the man in question (in my play) may have been a tinker or tramp, sailor, cattle drover—God knows what—types with which no priest would dream of interfering.

Tell Miss G.—or whoever it may be—that what I write of Irish country life I know to be true and I most emphatically will not change a syllable of it because A., B. or C. may think they know better than I do. The other speech you refer to is not fresh in my mind. We can discuss it when we meet. You understand my position: I am *quite ready* to avoid hurting people's feelings needlessly, but I will *not* falsify what I believe to be true for anybody. If one began that where would one end? I would rather drop play-writing altogether.

I told Miss G. today on the spur of the moment that the said man in the side ditch was a Protestant and that if the priest had touched him he would have got six months with hard labour for common assault—perhaps as good an answer as any, she seems to have thought that I was sneering at the priest for not doing his obvious duty, an idea which of course never entered my head.

If there are passages in the saint's role that give unnecessary trouble, I will do what I can to make them better if the reading committee—or if that is not possible you yourself—will point them out to me. Excuse scrawl and believe me very sincerely yours, J. M. Synge. P.S. Don't imagine for a moment that I am in any way annoyed at your note. On the contrary I am glad to know what is thought."

Miss G. was perhaps Miss Garvey who was not in the cast of "The Well of the Saints" though she played in the same programme as Sibby in "A Pot of Broth". Under the famous rule 6, however, she had as much right as anybody else in the Society to complain about plays or parts of plays put on at the Abbey. Synge's impatience with her was characteristic but it seemed a bit indiscreet to tease her about priests.

He watched rehearsals carefully, as he always did when he could, and took notes. One scribbled sheet of pencil notes on "The Well of the Saints" survives and contains useful comments which could be of practical use to a modern producer. "Timmy's key-note" he scribbles "is that he's always telling queer things and the lot of them nothing at all—thus he runs up before all the others to hear the news—when the saint appears he comes forward with a long speech about Martin and M. and so on—He is a good-natured naive, busybody with a hot temper—*i.e.,* that is how I felt him, but of course it is quite possible that in the necessarily slight sketch of him this did not come out strongly enough to tell on the stage."

Another note on character: "If it is possible—Timmy, Molly, should be got to show that in all their relations with Martin & Mary—friendly as they are—they feel their own superiority —for this reason Timmy's slapping Martin on the back, etc., is better left out."

And at last one, evidently written in the dark: "Getting up in the morning early, her food etc, permission and slow from that crescendo up to where he goes and stay up till he gets near and of course when it dies off a little the feeling having become so intense that it cannot be spoken."

The newspapers recorded that the first night audience for "The Well of the Saints" was not a crowded one and I have heard that there were fewer than fifty in the house ("no sixpenny seats, we told you so!"). The play was thought (by the "Irish Times") too literary without anything to give distraction from the long-drawn out dialogue—"Why not have a few good songs or instrumental pieces—Irish in flavour or Italian, or German, or French, or even English—to vary the evening's art pabulum?" One evening paper man frankly confessed the dilemma that most of the other critics were striving to conceal for, of course, they were supposed to be omniscient: The "Evening Mail" said "It is somewhat difficult accurately to 'place' Mr. Synge's work in dramatic literature, for although it is cast in dramatic manner it is not a play in the accepted sense of the word." His rival in the "Evening Herald" made a brave statement of critical ethics by reminding his readers that "On a recent occasion I disclaimed any intention of pronouncing on a play which I had not seen." He wondered why it was not possible to construct an Irish drama in which all the characters had "the regulation number of senses" and spoke up for just the sort of stage Irishman that the whole National Theatre idea was in conflict with—"The old type of whiskey-drinking, jig-dancing, Handy Rascal Pat Irishman manifested a certain boisterous and somewhat objectionable vivacity in and out of season . . . but I question if in most respects greatly the superior of the pessimistic loafer which there is a tendency to set up as a standard.

Once again a friend of the Abbey—though a rather ambiguous one—used the device of passing off a notice of the play as a letter to the editor. George Moore wrote to the "Irish Times" which printed it under the oddly-chosen headline of "Irish Literary Theatre", a lapse of memory perhaps, for that organisation had been disbanded. Moore felt it his duty to call attention of the readers to an important event which might be overlooked by them to their great regret. "The event I allude to is of exceeding rarity. I have never seen in London any play written originally in English that I can look upon as dramatic literature. I have not forgotten Oscar Wilde's plays—that delicious comedy "The Importance of Being Earnest," but however much I admire them I cannot forget that their style is derived from that of Restoration comedy, whereas Mr. Synge's little play seems to me of a new growth. Its apparent orthodoxy reminds us of the painters who worked in the latter half of the 15th century. . . . In your paper I would call attention to the abundance of beauty of the dialogue, to the fact that one listens as one listens to music, charmed by the inevitableness of the words and the ease with which phrase is linked to phrase. At every moment the dialogue seems to lose itself, but it finds its way out. Mr. Synge has discovered great literature in barbarous idiom as gold is discovered in quartz, and to do such a thing is surely a rare literary achievement. . . ."

Moore, at any rate, could see something shining through Synge's curious dialogue, something which escaped most of the professional critics, though Philip Carr in the "Manchester Guardian" described Synge's method as "direct and searching. His dialogue is at once natural and picturesque. It is founded on the speech of the Irish peasantry . . . Mr. Synge has used this speech as no Irish writer has used it before." In his own country, and especially among the Abbey actors it was, of course, realised that Synge was using speech in a way that no Irish peasant had ever used it at all, and Moore's simile of music was a particularly sound one, for Synge's dialogue is a composition in which words and rhythms are used in a way never dreamed of in everyday speech in any part of Ireland although the Irish have a mastery of English vocabulary which flatly contradicts the Gaelic theory that it is a foreign language to them and the speaking of it exerts a tension which in turns causes them to be at odds with their English neighbours.

Synge had a good start over any English playwright when it came to creating a rich, colourful dialogue for Irish-English is a rich colourful language to begin with. Synge-Irish-English, a unique dialect, has never been spoken properly anywhere but at the Abbey Theatre and the early players had to struggle to impose it on their natural way of speech. Willie Fay found it entirely a matter of mastering the rhythm of each sentence and he not only had to do this for himself but help others to find the key. Maire nic Shiubhlaigh believed that the style was arrived at by transcribing direct from the Gaelic of the Western Islands but this oversimplifies. Her description of the difficulty of speaking the lines of "In the Shadow of the Glen" is an excellent summary: "At first I found Synge's lines almost impossible to learn and deliver. Like the wandering ballad-singer I had to 'humour' them into a strange tune, changing the metre several times each minute. It was neither verse nor prose . . . every passage brought

G

some new difficulty and we would all stumble through the speeches until the tempo in which they were written was finally discovered. . . ."

It was neither verse nor prose, English nor translated Gaelic. What took a long, long time to sink in was that Synge's writing was the work of an original genius, and I use the word with no qualification. In its first season in its permanent home the Abbey Theatre had nurtured and presented a genius who was to be recognised in Europe then in the rest of the world before he was fully accepted in his own country. It had also introduced to Dublin a unique theatre—the first permanent subsidised one in the English-speaking world, later to become the first State endowed English speaking theatre in the British Commonwealth.

Chapter Seven

FIRST SEASONS

THE first Abbey season continued with Lady Gregory's "Kincora" in March, William Boyle's comedy "The Building Fund" in April and Padraic Colum's "The Land" in June. The staging of so many new plays, with revivals now and then, by a small amateur company still organised as a dramatic society was proving difficult. The first change made brought to a head once more the difference between professionals and amateurs. There were in the Society several ambitious young people who saw in the Abbey the chance of a professional career and there were those to whom any such ambition was a betrayal of either a national or an artistic ideal. Whatever the dangers it might bring up, however, it was decided to disband the Irish National Theatre Society in the autumn of 1905 and replace it by the National Theatre Society, Ltd. This seemed a small alteration, but it was a radical one and some of the members had deep misgivings. Padraic Colum was one of them and before long he was writing to Yeats to say "As you are aware I voted for the establishment of a limited liability company in order to save the Society from a disastrous split. I come back to Dublin and find the Society hopelessly shattered. The one thing to be done is to re-unite the society. Until this is done the dramatic movement is hung up. I appeal to you—I earnestly appeal to you to take steps to re-unite the groups." But the shattering did not take place immediately and there was time to impose a new pattern on the theatre. When the Society became a limited company the executive power had to be put in the hands of

99

directors. Synge, Yeats and Lady Gregory were appointed and the first change in relationship was that the players and the small stage staff, who had been fellow-members in a society, became, overnight, employees. It was at this point that one of the bad mistakes of the early years was made: not one actor or actress was on the board—one of the Fays might have been a logical choice to perform some special duties as an expert witness when questions directly affecting the players had to be discussed. But it did not happen and one of the seeds of future dissolution was unthinkingly sown.

Another profound change was the payment of salaries to several of the company. Willie Fay was already receiving £2 a week (two years later his contract gave him £2 as actor and £2 as producer). Frank Fay was still working at Craig, Gardner but decided to give up his job when the directors offered him 30s. a week to become a professional actor, and others joined him. Willie Fay reported to Yeats early in September: "I had an interview with Moyra Walker (Maire nic Shiubhlaigh) last night and she is willing to take the moneyed engagement, but reckoned that her brother (Frank Walker) was worth more than 10s. and of course I think they are all worth more but we are too hard up to give it. But as she seemed very anxious that he should be along with her I said that I am sure we could promise him the 15s. the same as the others. I suppose the odd 5 shillings wont make a great deal of difference in the guarantee and it is worth a bit to secure the two of them . . . I feel sure that after a bit the actors under salary will be quite ready to have the life of anyone that tries to keep them back . . . I suppose you see my point about the voting, that you can't pay anyone for doing certain work and then vote him in or out. You can only work it on agreement and a notice on either side to terminate it . . . I would be glad to know if you think we ought to start payment on 1st Oct or 1st Nov, for these people will in some cases have to give notice, the brother will have to give a month's, and there is no use making the agreements till we are quite decided who are to be the responsible people for the regular payment of them which as far as I see would be best paid on Saturdays—same as the ordinary theatres, a weekly payment terminable by a fortnight's notice on either side."

Here again more mischief was brewing for the future for, in the end, it was over the question of who should be responsible for hiring and firing the company that the incurable breach between Willie Fay and the Directors took place. As General Manager of the Abbey he was often in conflict with Yeats on matters of immediate policy; he usually got his own way, and where the question was one of staging or acting he was generally right. He was less patient in his letter-writing than his brother (he left most of the correspondence to Frank) and there is a sharp note every now and then which almost echoes Synge when roused. When there was some difference of opinion about whether a play was fit for production Willie Fay wrote to Yeats saying no change could be made because the printing was already in hand. "What is the use of bothering about what people say?" he asked "they will say what they like without consulting our wishes on the matter. Boyle is the nearest approach to a new piece we have, only been played three nights and then when most of our people were away. Colum will I feel sure draw on reputation and talk. Let us when we decide on a thing carry it out and take the consequences good or bad. Nothing makes a place weaker than wobbling about from one thing to another, it leaves a feeling of uncertainty always hovering over the place."

"All art is a collaboration" Synge wrote in his introduction to "The Playboy of the Western World" and in the Abbey in its first year collaboration was very much in the air. Frank Fay was invited to become formally a teacher of verse speaking and voice production so that he could help the other players to develop their natural talents. Yeats, offering him an extra ten shillings a week, wrote "I always look upon you as the most beautiful verse speaker I know—at least you and Mrs. Emery compete together in my mind for that—and I know nobody but you who can teach verse speaking."

Collaboration of a different sort is illustrated by a three-sided correspondence between Willie Fay, Yeats and Synge on the merits and demerits of William Boyle's "The Building Fund" (originally called "The Coming of Shiela"). Fay found it vulgar but did not believe this really serious because it was about "the most essentially vulgar people in the country" (which seems rather hard on the Louth farmers). He advised very strongly

against asking Colum to help Boyle out of his difficulties—for
one thing he was in difficulties enough of his own with his next
play "The Land" and for another Fay thought Boyle would
not like it "considering he has lived ten years in the country for
Colum's one, and knows it." He suggested that either Yeats or
Synge ought to lend a hand. Synge, who was staying with a
Mrs. Harris at Mountain Stage, Glenbeigh, Co. Kerry, wrote:
"I'm sorry I have been so long in answering your letter. I have
had several moves, and in these places it is not easy to get a quiet
place to write. I sent you Boyle's play some time ago and I hope
it reached you safely. I also wrote Yeats my opinion of it in brief.
I have not much more to say of it for good or bad. I think it
has a great deal of vitality but it is not possible in its present
state, though I think a little revision would make it possible.
. . . There is the most terrible rain going on here now and the
thatch is dripping and splashing about my ears, in spite of tin
buckets stuck about the floor to catch the drops. A letter and
any news would now be an infinite blessing to yours cordialement,
J. M. Synge."

There is no sign that Boyle knew about aspersions on his
play being passed to and fro. He went to London and sent
back for a copy of the typescript so that he could go about
securing his American copyright and he asked Maunsel & Co.
to wait a while before printing it because he might want "to
alter a word here and there".

When the play was produced it was a credit to whoever did
the necessary doctoring. Indeed it still reads well and could be
revived. The "Freeman's Journal" said that it "scintillates
with epigrams and persiflage" but the "Leader" found the
Abbey rather a wilderness and thought the Saturday night
audience the smallest yet in "that, so far, ill-fated theatre".
Still harping on Miss Horniman's "snobbery" its critic suggested
"As in Russia, the best way to inaugurate reform and restore
public confidence might be by an extension of the franchise.
Let in the sixpenny moujik and the people will begin to take
hope, and feel that the day of oligarchy is at an end."

In his autobiography Willie Fay described 1903 as the *annus
mirabilis* of the National Theatre Society. That certainly could
not be claimed for 1905 for although it was the first full year

of the Society's own theatre it was an unprofitable one financially and the responsibility of trying not to draw on Miss Horniman's £600 a year guarantee for salaries made it essential to stop the drain of steady box office losses. The obvious choice seemed to be to wade even deeper into professionalism and to play not only in full sized theatres but to take the company "on tour". In 1904 and 1905 Miss Horniman had spent £2,000 altogether on the building and subsidy. The 1905 figure was to be £2,309, after which there was a sharp decline—1906, £932; 1907, £703; 1908, £655; 1909, £150. A document marked in her own handwriting "Whole expenses of the Abbey Scheme" gives a total of £9,957 17s. 2d., but as she also paid the losses on tours in Britain the exact total is difficult to arrive at.

The first tour, in the winter of 1905, was to quite a large extent managed by Miss Horniman herself, and when it turned out impossible to arrange for commercial managers to take the company in at Oxford and Cambridge she booked the Corn Exchange, Oxford and in Cambridge the Victoria Assembly Rooms for an evening performance and the Small Guildhall for a matinee. There was also another opportunity to play before the London critics. The English newspaper comment was most gratifying but there was no big profit. Miss Horniman then decided that more might be expected from a tour of the "number one" towns of the United Kingdom. It was planned in two parts, first a visit in April (1906) to Manchester, Liverpool and Leeds, then a summer trip covering Cardiff, Aberdeen, Edinburgh, Glasgow and Newcastle-on-Tyne. The first part of the tour produced a loss of £200. Leeds was a miserable town for the company, for they spent £55 18s. 6d. on expenses and took £5 10s. 11d. from a handful of audience. The highest takings (£28) and the highest expenses (£70) were in Manchester.

I have not seen the figures for the second half of the tour, but whatever its financial result, it was a fateful one for the Abbey Theatre for it began Miss Horniman's campaign to rid the theatre of the Fays. She fought tooth and nail, unsuccessfully, for almost two years and produced the atmosphere in which after prolonged argument and some recrimination the Fays left Dublin. There could be no question of Miss Horniman's sincerity, no question that there would not have been an Abbey

Theatre without her, but she seemed to choose as her targets just those who could do most good for the theatre—she disliked Synge, Maire O'Neill and Sarah Allgood only a little less than she did Willie Fay.

Her agitation began in January 1906 and her first line of attack was that the theatre needed a more highly paid, and therefore more professionally trained manager than Willie Fay. Yeats suggested going about the change in a diplomatic way, but that did not go down well. She wrote from Tunis, beginning her letter as she always did, "My dear demon" and with hardly any preamble was straight into the attack: "If I thought Fay 'capable' why should I offer to pay another man? 'An Irish toy' is, I consider, the right name for what now exists, but I ask nobody to agree with me. This is not a case for 'diplomacy' as I cannot fight Fay with his own weapons; he is so unscrupulous in his vanity and Mr. Synge is under his thumb . . . If you only get the new man accepted by 'diplomacy' he wont be allowed to be of any use and will simply cause a waste of money. You yourself *know* that the scheme is only a toy at present. The public agree voicelessly, let the other directors say what they may. That I want him (Fay) left to do what he is capable of doing should shew that I have no spite against him. Yours, Annie."

There was not the slightest reason why Miss Horniman should have any spite against either of the Fays, or anybody else in the company or on the board of directors. But it is difficult not to read some of her letters as malicious. She began bombarding Yeats with complaints about the management of the company and its conduct on tour. She wrote a memorandum on the subject of noisy conduct, recording that she had been scolded at the Trevelyan Hotel, Leeds, because a tin trumpet was being blown at two in the morning. The same trumpet, she said would have been (but for her firmness) played through the streets of Leeds the next day. She guessed that the only person who was able to sleep on the journey between Cardiff and Glasgow was Alfred Wareing, who was deaf.

Wareing was not the "other man" Miss Horniman was so anxious to find as a replacement for Willie Fay. He was with the company as a temporary touring manager (his wife lending a general hand) and was valuable for negotiating terms with tough theatre owners. When it came to bargaining he could do better, even in Irish country towns, than any of the company and his success strenghtened Miss Horniman's belief that somebody from the commercial theatre, trained in the ways of the profession, was needed to take care of the Abbey Theatre.

Apart from her complaints about conduct, the first part of the tour went well, but Miss Horniman was soon sending communiques of what amounted to a civil war between her and Willie Fay. Synge's version of what seems to have been the worst row was even more vivid than Miss Horniman's. He wrote it to Lady Gregory: "Things . . . are not going very smoothly. Mrs. Wareing as I suppose you heard went off to London and they got down a Mr. Bell to replace her, a profoundly self-satisfied and vulgar commercial man, that none of us can abide. He got Miss H. more or less into his hands, and at last she sailed round to Fay one evening just before the show to suggest that Bell should 'make up' the company. Fay broke out forthwith and she describes her exit as that of 'a stage cat driven out of the kitchen with a broomstick'. She complains pathetically to me that everyone in Glasgow knows that she is paying for our show and that she feels in a rather foolish position when she has to confess that she has no authority over it! We will have to be very careful indeed about our next step. I am not writing much to Yeats while he is with Miss Horniman, he is so careless about his letters."

There was also trouble about accounts, about the petty cash, about bills being paid from the wrong fund, and so on. ". . . This has annoyed me very much" Miss Horniman wrote from Edinburgh. "I feel as if whatever we do will be frittered away unless Fay comes to the conclusion that the Directors must direct. I am going to keep out of the way of the company as I am very anxious not to be the excuse for any further disagreeableness. . . . As I have always said it is for the whole movement, not individuals, that we must act and if Fay insists on overdoing the part of the old-fashioned Prima Donna, he *must* be brought to his senses."

The next day she was telling Yeats of a plan "maturing in my mind by which there will be Home Rule in the Abbey Theatre." As long as there were two authorities she believed

". . . Fay will try to set them at logger-heads and so get his own way." She proposed to put the purse strings in the hands of the Directors by paying her subsidy to them in a lump sum instead of releasing it herself when needed. This would certainly avoid unpleasant notes like the one she sent about a sum of £50 needed for stage equipment. ". . . I refuse to send it to Fay to be dribbled away without any account being rendered to me. I do not ask Fay for detailed accounts, only the bare fact that he wants more and how much is left and an acknowledgment of what I send."

She asked that her "home rule" plan should be carefully thought over by Yeats so that he could be prepared to discuss it seriously when they next met. "I cannot and will not have your powers wasted over silly rows" she wrote "when you should be doing *great* work. This letter please is purely a proposal made so as to give you full power over the theatre. I must not stand in your light in any way. You understand my attitude, I hope; that I think of your advantage and your fame."

The next day, without waiting for any further discussion she had decided that her only possible course of action was to resign all connection with the theatre and simply hand over the money to the directors. "I have been virtually dismissed by Fay and as the performances are absolutely under his control the only way I can practically help the Directors is by putting the power of the purse into their hands. . . ."

Again, next day, there was another letter in a series which must have been a great burden to Yeats, but now Miss Horniman had calmed down a little and felt much relieved in her mind by the decision to put everything in the hands of the directors. "It would have been impossible for me to keep Fay on as my representative after he was so rude. Apart from that interview [presumably in his dressing room] he had gone on obstructing me in so many ways that were most foolish . . . you will have to get someone to see after the business matters because other-wise *your* time and strength will be wasted." If the other half of the correspondence had been preserved it would be possible to know exactly what Yeats's reaction to this bombardment was. It is just feasible to read between the lines of Miss Horniman's letters that she did not get much encouragement. She went so far in one letter as to drop the cosiness of "My Dear Demon" and the friendly signature "Annie"; her complaint this time began "Dear Mr. Yeats" and ended "yours sincerely A. E. F. Horniman". The theme was the same as the others.

Synge had a much less dramatic explanation of any temporary shortcomings there might be in Willie Fay's work: "W. G. Fay, by the way, is not good just now as he is much occupied with his love affairs." Perhaps younger people in love were upsetting to Miss Horniman, for she also seemed waspish about Synge: she wrote to her Demon "Fay encouraged the Molly Allgood [Maire O'Neill] business and the rowdiness at Leeds too. Of course Mr. Synge is willing to give her up now—three months of one girl on his knee doubtless leads him to wish for a change."

There was grievous misunderstanding between her and the high spirited young Irish girls into whose company she was thrown by the long journeys of a provincial tour. There was no common ground between them at all and little chance of people from two such different worlds settling down together even with a common passion for the theatre to help them.

Neither of the Fays could have suspected what was being said about them by Miss Horniman, though apparently Synge had a very clear notion and was disinclined to follow the anti-Fay line, which is no doubt one of the reasons why Miss Horniman despised him so. She invited Yeats and Lady Gregory to prove that her forebodings about the company were falsely founded: ". . . But you must not reckon on Mr. Synge" she added "He feels that Fay's nerves and fads and fancies are of more importance than our status in the eyes of the public. He can't help it, I scarcely blame him. You told me that he allowed me to speak in Ireland in a way that he did not like and yet made no demur and I called it cowardice. Every bitter thing I have said about Ireland has been put into my mind by my experiences among your people, am I to blame for that?"

Her clash with the Irish temperament was inevitable, for she was not able to distinguish between the different types of Irish men and women she had to deal with. In fixing on the Fays, the Allgoods and Synge as the root of what she thought to be evils she was certainly unjust. She particularly misunderstood Willie Fay, for when she accused him of slovenliness on the stage she was referring to an acting style which others believed

showed the touch of genius. It was even more unjust for her to
say that he hated: ". . . the honest hard-working professional
life" and sought "an excuse to be lazy and slovenly whilst you
want even greater care and greater loyalty to Art." He had
done some very hard graft touring Britain and Ireland with third,
fourth or fifth rate little companies while learning the elements
of his craft; and he loved every moment of it simply because it
was a hardworking, professional and in his eyes adventurous
life. The misunderstanding between him and Miss Horniman
on what was "commercial" and what "artistic" seemed insoluble.
Willie Fay believed, and said so in his autobiography, that he
and Miss Horniman were in accord in trying to make the Abbey
into an "Art theatre". They were both people of sharp temper,
which may have added to the confusion—and Synge was hot
tempered too. "I am as excitable as you are" he wrote to Willie
Fay during the English tour "so that when we take to arguing
in public its the Divil!" Miss Horniman's attitude towards
Synge was a little more complicated. He was a fellow director,
however repulsive, and a gentleman, however wayward. He
was one of the supermen, Fay one of the slaves: so Synge had
to be tolerated, at least on the surface, though he could always
be abused (to another fellow director) in delicate terms like:
"He is afraid of Fay and so toadied to him; I can use no other
word."

For the time being, Miss Horniman was not winning any
real allies. Lady Gregory was cool about a suggestion to bring
in a professional from England who would cost four or five
hundred pounds a year. "At present," she wrote "I don't feel
that I can give a definite opinion. The one thing I hold to is
that the Fays should not be put out either by forcible or gradual
means." Synge felt the same and there is no evidence at this time
of a strong desire by Yeats to interfere with the Fay methods
of running the Abbey even in the face of a more than usually
violent attack from Miss Horniman in which she included this
fine passage of invective:

"Lady Gregory and Mr. Synge grovel at Fay's feet. They
sacrifice your work and keep you a bond-slave to them because
you are 'touched' by that vampire Kathleen ni Houlihan . . .
they only care to shew themselves off to a small set in Dublin

at my expense without caring for anything beyond their own vanity. Now try to put yourself into the place of some decent person who cares for the drama and does not care a rap for hole and corner 'Irish ideas'; he would say—'why on earth should the woman who cares for Art stint her daily life forever for a local affair which is run in a way which cannot lead to anything of artistic result? Why should she be bullied and fleeced by people who 'diplomatically' snub her in every possible way? Why should she not try something else where she may not be insulted at every turn?

"You are ceaselessly victimised by Lady Gregory on the score of your gratitude for her kindness. You are being made a slave, your genius is put under a net in that precious 'garden' and you are only let out when you are wanted to get something out of *me*."

The fangs show there, all right, and something of the personal feeling between the two women is forced up to the surface by Miss Horniman's indignation. She made little headway yet a while; but within a year of her bringing the campaign to the boil the Fays were on the way out, and within two years there was no longer any place for her in the Abbey scheme of things and she was off to more sympathetic (though no more profitable) ground in Manchester.

A new season began in October, 1906, with "The Gaol Gate," and "Spreading the News" both by Lady Gregory; and "The Mineral Workers" by William Boyle. The plays went well though some home truths delivered by Boyle caused hissing from the pit. Yet there was nothing offensive in "The Mineral Workers" and the conflict it illustrated between agriculture and industry exists just as strongly in the Ireland of today; so does the mistrust of anybody who proposes to interfere too much with the natural order of things. But hissing at the Abbey or sniping in the political weeklies had little to do with the merits or arguments of the plays.

There was a sensitiveness growing up which is often the result of a developing nationalism. Stephen Gwynn illustrated it excellently in a dialogue between a plain Irishman and a Gaelic Leaguer: "Did you ever hear that song they call 'Phil the Fluter's Ball'?" the plain man asks, and the Gaelic Leaguer replies with conscious virtue, and possibly with a little untruth "No, indeed, I never did." "I'm asking you" says the plain man "because there's a cry out against me letting it be sung at a concert. And I tell you now I see nothing in it but fun, honest Irish fun." At which the Gaelic Leaguer gives the whole game away by saying "That may be quite true. But still you see, we aren't a country in an ordinary condition, and there are many things that are harmless enough in themselves but that would have a bad effect on the people, if we were to be laughing over them in public." In other words, to build up a national dignity it is sometimes necessary to suppress the truth or to present only selected aspects of it.

Bernard Shaw obviously affected to believe that some such obscurantism was at work over "John Bull's Other Island" when he said to a reporter "Here's a play by an Irishman on Ireland as original as anything could be, as sympathetic with the genius of the people and in every way racy of the soil. Why don't the National Theatre people give it? Shall I tell you? Well, one reason is that the blinding of naked truth in that outburst of an English valet would so enrage all Nationalist auditors that they'd rise as one man at it, and burn the house down." This made a good headline but there was no truth in it. The play had been offered to the Abbey before it was given to Granville Barker for production in London. The first objection, and it was a serious one, was that there was no actor in the Abbey company who could have made even a reasonable shot at Broadbent.

When he saw it at the Court Theatre, Yeats was relieved, because although he had waited for a long time (he had heard from Shaw about it even when the play was just an idea) he found it disappointing—shapeless, fundamentally ugly, but worst of all interminable. The matinee began at 2.30 and ended at 6 and this was, as C. B. Purdom notes in the "Shaw—Barker Letters", after very heavy cuts indeed had been made during rehearsals. Purdom also makes it perfectly clear that Shaw followed the casting of "John Bull" more closely than any reasonable author would be expected to and his remarks on the experienced and talented actors brought forward for consideration suggest that it would have been hard to satisfy him with the small choice offered in Dublin.

Yeats thought nothing of the suggestion that "John Bull's Other Island" would offend the Nationalists. "We've offended the susceptibilities of so many parties," he said "that we are really deserving of a reputation for courage. If we had performed Shaw's play we would not have made any cuts to modify his point of view. Every writer is entitled to his point of view."

If there was any doubt about the Abbey's being able to offend many parties it was about to be dispelled. "Deirdre" by W. B. Yeats was given a first production in November, 1906, followed by "The Shadowy Waters" and Lady Gregory's "The Canavans" in December; the next to be put into rehearsal was "The Playboy of the Western World". While this was going on a change was being made in Willie Fay's position. The new manager was to come in; Fay was to be given an additional £100 a year to act as producer for all Irish dialect plays (which Miss Horniman called 'peasant' plays), was to have a contract, and was to step down only in a limited way. The new man, Synge believed "will have to have more business than stage management and it is essential that he should be a thorough theatrical *business* man, if possible an Irishman." He impressed on Yeats the need for the "new man" to co-operate with and help Willie Fay in the friendliest way—better to wait rather than to bring over the wrong man who would make a mess of it; but most important of all from Synge's point of view: "The Playboy is going very well in rehearsal and for the time all is smooth. Please *do not* bring or send over new man till the Playboy is over as it is *absolutely* essential that Fay should be undisturbed till he has got through this big part."

Chapter Eight

"PLAYBOY" BATTLE

THE internal troubles of the Abbey were shelved for a while, for the theatre was on the verge of its greatest battle, the "Playboy Riots" and some people seemed to know it. Willie Fay foresaw some of the dangers of the "Playboy" text and warned Synge that the use of certain words might cause trouble. A few changes were made in the text but on the whole Synge stuck to the principle that he had laid down over "The Well of the Saints"—that he would say what he believed to be the truth, or give up writing plays altogether. The "Playboy" had cost him more labour than anything he had done before, he had written and re-written it through several versions before refining it down to the text he presented for rehearsal at the Abbey. It used the name of God rather freely (a sufficiently well-known Irish characteristic, God knows) and contained one word which was to put part of the audience into a fine frenzy—the word was "shift" and when the troubles of January 26th, 1907, and the later nights are described now, fifty years later, it is usually thought necessary to define "shift". It is the feminine of shirt, a chemise, a basic undergarment for women, long obsolete. It would have taken remarkable foresight to realise during the rehearsals that this word among so many others would prove one of the chief trouble-makers of the play. Arthur Griffith tried to make out that expressions even fouler than "bloody" and "shift" were used on the stage, but agreed in the end that they did not appear in the script. Sarah Allgood was accused of using the word ". . . indicating an essential item of female attire which the lady would probably never utter in ordinary circumstances, even to herself." Willie Fay was able to quote an anonymous poem from the "Evening Mail" which he believed was written by Susan Mitchell, "A.E.'s" secretary who was responsible for a whole anthology of epigrams attributed to her in the way that certain "Churchillisms" are attributed to Sir Winston. My two favourite verses are:

> Unless we watch your wanton text,
>   And waken shame with boos and knockings,
> You'll want that poor Miss Allgood next
>   To mention st—ck—ngs.

> Unless we curb from hour to hour
>   This frenzied cult of Aphrodite
> You'll urge reluctant Ambrose Power
>   To name his n—ghty.

It would seem in retrospect, especially to those who do not understand the Irish temperament that the whole row over the "Playboy" was merely a sign of infantilism in public opinion. But it went much deeper than that. "Bloody" and "shift" did not cause audiences to break up in disorder, to fight with fists, to attempt attacks on the actors, to struggle with the police and above all to keep up such a constant hullabaloo that after the first night hardly a word of the "Playboy" was heard again, in a week of performances, except when silence was imposed by the police. It was not a too frequent repetition of the name of God that made William Boyle withdraw his popular plays "The Building Fund", "The Mineral Workers" and "The Eloquent Dempsey" from the Abbey repertory as a protest. It was not even entirely an unaided explosion of wrath which was touched off by the idea that an Irish girl would fall in love with a known and boastful parricide. There were many elements in the "Playboy riots"—and whatever may have been said afterwards the contemporary accounts, and the recollections of those who were there, confirm the fact that the word "riot" was no exaggeration.

The hostility of the Nationalists towards the Abbey had been growing but the attack, on the political front, had not

H

been particularly successful, though a few faithful supporters had been enticed away. A much more fruitful line of attack might be to use the smear of "immorality". In his "The Irish Drama" (1929) Andrew E. Malone made no bones about it at all. "This attack became narrowed", he wrote "and focussed on a definite object when Synge's 'In the Shadow of the Glen' was produced in October 1903. This new attack upon the Theatre was opened in the daily press, but soon the organ of Sinn Fein, 'The United Irishman', which had once supported the dramatic movement, joined in the attack, and from this time onward criticised adversely almost every play produced by the Theatre. It was especially hostile to Synge who was accused of being 'a French decadent', and to this consistently hostile propaganda in an influential periodical can be traced the beginnings of the riot which greeted the first production of 'The Playboy of the Western World' four years later.

"I was brought to the theatre for a purpose" one of the accused said in a Dublin police court. "I came here to protest against the play." Who brought him? Were there any others among the audience who were not there of their own pure volition? It is too much to believe, knowing the nature of Irish politics, that the caterwauling in the Abbey was entirely spontaneous. It was not all even one-sided for youths from Trinity College joined in and made the confusion worse by singing "God save the King" in the stalls to drown "God Save Ireland" from the pit. They came in parties, having marched out of the College gate and across the Liffey to the Abbey.

On Saturday, January 26th, the curtain went up on Flaherty's public-house on a dark autumn evening on a wild coast of Mayo and Pegeen mulled over her shopping list. The play went well at first and there were plenty of laughs. But soon the mood of the audience began to change and there was some hissing and booing, and an angry shout or two before the end, an altercation after the final curtain. But that was about all on the first night. The newspapers were not unanimous by any means. The "Independent" noted that "a crowded, brilliant and discriminating audience paid tribute to the players, whatever may have been the general feelings as to the merits of the play." The "Evening Mail" man wrote: "Mr. Synge may have been pulling our

leg with his theme, and we are not going to gratify him with
indignation. But we do resent it when, having given proof of
brilliant powers of dialogue, he deliberately assails our ears
with coarse or blasphemous language." The "Freeman's Journal"
could not bring itself to print in full some of the things it objected to and raved: "Everything is a b—y this or a b—y that
and into this picturesque dialogue names that should only be
used with respect and reverence are frequently introduced.
Enough! The hideous caricature would be slanderous of a Kaffir
kraal. The piece is announced to run for a week: it is to be hoped
it will be instantly withdrawn."

There were some letters to editors but on the whole the press
reception was not violent, any more than the first night itself
had been. But the real trouble began on the Monday. The
house was not full, but the cheaper seats were packed—and
perhaps packed in more senses than one. As soon as Christy
Mahon made it clear that he had "killed his da" the restless-
ness began; it grew as Pegeen and the girls appeared to admire
Christy for his courage and it erupted beyond control when
it was decided that Pegeen might spend the night in Flaherty's
shebeen with nobody to keep her company but Christy, the
Playboy and parricide. Here the real uproar began, with stamping,
shouting, singing, beating of the floor and the seats with sticks.
The players could no longer be heard and it is not much of an
exaggeration to say that scarcely a word of Synge was heard
from that moment to the end of the run.

Yeats was still away in Scotland, where on the Saturday
he had received Lady Gregory's pungent telegram: "Audience
broke up in disorder at the word shift." But she was there again
and so was Synge. Although they were both directors it was
left to Willie Fay, who was struggling with his biggest piece
of creative work since the Abbey began, to stop the performance
and walk down to the footlights and ask for a hearing. The
exchange, in part, went like this:
Mr. Fay: "There are people here who have paid to see the piece.
Anyone who does not like the play can have his money returned."
Cries of "We dont want the money. It is a libel on the National
Theatre. We never expected this of the Abbey." (Tumultuous
applause, mixed with cries of 'Sinn Fein for ever').

A Voice: "Such a thing as is represented could not occur in Ireland."

Mr. Fay: "You have not won. I will send for the police, and every man who kicks up a row will be removed."

Cries of "Send for them. We will meet them."

At this point the curtain was brought down and the audience cheered more wildly than ever, for they believed they had won and had stopped the "Playboy".

But in a few minutes the tune changed radically and shouts of victory were replaced by cries of incredulity, for the threat had been carried out: A dozen policemen marched in and stood around, looking as policemen do in such circumstances. Others patrolled outside the theatre. The booing broke out again, but the curtain went up and Willie Fay again spoke, repeating his offer of money back to whoever did not like the play. This was greeted with more shouts of "We're not afraid", "We won't have it" and the like. But the players began once more trying to finish the first act. The Freeman's Journal description of it said "Amidst boohing and other conceivable and almost inconceivable noises, the action of the drama was proceeded with. It was mere dumbshow as far as the artistes were concerned. Not a syllable they spoke could be heard. At last the curtain descended on the conclusion of the first section of the production, amidst howls, cheers and the singing of national songs.

"Now the unexpected occurred. As the result of some apparently mystic sign or command the constables turned right about and marched in a stately style out of the building. Needless is it to state that the victorious occupants of the pit and gallery signalised their success by triumphant yells, shouts, tramping of feet and belabouring of seats and walls with sturdy sticks, mingled with the singing of 'The West's Awake', 'A Nation Once Again' and such like well-known patriotic compositions in which nearly all the audience joined.

"At ten o'clock the curtain was raised on the second act. Once more the performance was merely pantomimic owing to the hurricane of hissing with which it was greeted.

"A similar fate awaited the presentation of the third act.

"For fully five minutes after the play had concluded the

building was the scene of great animation and excitement. Those who had objected to the entertainment gave effect to their elation in energetic outbursts in both Irish and English on the success they had achieved and energetically declared that they would adopt a similar attitude on every occasion the play would be produced. Mr. Fay, in the middle of the closing exciting incidents, came forward and said—'Those people who are here tonight will say, 'We heard this play—' (cries of 'we have heard enough') during which Mr. Fay retired."

Although they made less fuss about the calling in of the police other newspapers of January 29th support this account. I give the date because exactly what happened during the first week of the "Playboy" seems to have become vague in the minds of those who were there. Maire nic Shiubhlaigh says it was on the third night that the police were called in and that they came after W. B. Yeats had made a speech pleading with the sensible members of the audience to remain quiet. Willie Fay in his autobiography said "It was not until the Thursday night that, in order to give a fair deal to those who had paid their money to hear, the directors had the police in the theatre." He does not mention having himself appealed to the audience to be quiet and having threatened that the police would be sent for. They were in several times during the week and arrests were made in the theatre but it is perfectly clear that they were first called on Monday, January 28th. By whom? Hone in his life of Yeats says that Lady Gregory sent for them and that it was also she who sent out an S.O.S., through her son Robert, to Trinity College. Whether or not she sent for them Lady Gregory said very firmly that it was at her request and Mr. Synge's that the police withdrew: she also said, with a splendid disregard for what we now call "public relations" that "in the opinion of those conducting this theatre it is the fiddler who chooses the tune. The public are quite at liberty to stay away, but if they come they must take what is provided for them."

Yeats was not in the theatre on the night that the police first came in, but later in the week he was responsible for their being called again. The first person publicly to threaten police action was Willie Fay. The first to ask the police to leave was Lady Gregory. Does it all matter? Well not now, perhaps, but it did at the time, for the Dublin Metropolitan Police were regarded, just as much as the Royal Irish Constabulary as instruments of British oppression and calling them in to the National Theatre was giving the Nationalists a powerful weapon of propaganda against the Abbey.

A lot of the indignation about the play, its language and its theme, was whipped up and exaggerated. Some of this was the work of Arthur Griffith and the "United Irishman", though just as he left his columns open to contrary views, Griffith was ready enough to correct himself publicly if necessary. He wrote to a newspaper withdrawing his suggestion that "a certain low expression" had been used from the stage and agreed that he had seen it in the text and that he accepted the actor's assurance that the word he used was, as printed, "stuttering". But no whipping up was required to make any Dublin crowd with a high proportion of nationalists in it furious at the sight of the blue uniforms which they regarded just as British as the scarlet tunics of the soldiers, mostly of the Irish regiments in the British army, who were to be seen proudly walking in the streets of Dublin with girls on their arms.

By the Friday night, after some arrests had been made, the performance went in comparative quietness, but only because the walls of the auditorium were lined with police who acted quickly against interrupters.

Synge, throughout, showed a haughty disdain of the audiences which was not designed to make him loved the more. "I don't care a rap" was his first reaction when interviewed. He asserted that the play was an extravaganza and that he never cared whether his plots were typically Irish or not. But to another reporter he showed more signs of wanting to justify himself. He said that the idea of the play was suggested to him by the fact that a few years ago a man who committed a murder was kept hidden by the people on one of the Arran Islands until he could get off to America. He also picked up some hints from the chase of Lynchehaun who was a brutal murderer of a woman but who with the aid of his neighbours managed to conceal himself from the police for months and in the end to get away to safety.

The accusation that a play was a slander on the fair name of Ireland was not a novelty: it had been heard before, especially about Synge, and was to be heard again especially about O'Casey. There were many at the time who not only saw the quality of Synge but who also saw through the demonstrations as having other motives than merely keeping the stage of Dublin pure. A good witness was Denis Brogan, father of Professor D. W. Brogan. He heard all around him, during one of the noisiest performances, shouts that no such thing could happen in Ireland. But Brogan, although he was a Gaelic enthusiast, took a minority view. He never tired of telling his friends about the man from his own village who was known as "Bagdad". This was not only because he had lived in the Middle East but also because, infuriated at his father's longevity and the delay in inheriting the family farm, he had shot the old man with both barrels of a shot-gun. He succeeded only in winging his da (as Christy Mahon did too) but his attempt, Mr. Brogan used to say, was a well-known practice among the peasantry.

Synge knew all about this; so did his detractors. Synge knew about cruelty and superstition and meanness and lying and disloyalty and murder and bastardy; but in the bright lexicon of Sinn Fein there were no such words, except so far as they could be applied to the British. It is a failing of national movements that they must never admit a truth which lessens the nobility of their common people. The root of the matter was dragged up (as it so often was) by Bernard Shaw, who said in New York that the American Fenian organisation Clan-na-Gael ". . . suddenly struck out the brilliant idea that to satirise the follies of humanity is to insult the Irish nation, because the Irish nation is, in fact, the human race and has no follies and stands there pure and beautiful and saintly to be eternally oppressed by England and collected for by the Clan."

Stephen Gwynn called the campaign against the "Playboy" a contest of lungs against brains but it was much more than that. It was a contest of propaganda against play-writing, of the belief that art is not for art's sake but for the national interest, against the attitude that means and end are inseparable and sacrosanct in any artistic pursuit. The first attitude produces the sort of artistic sterility that Stalinism did in Russia; but the second is equally dangerous for it tends to produce "Waiting for Godot" or examples of the welder's craft, like "The Unknown Political Prisoner", passed off as sculpture.

Whether or not Synge believed he had written a play with a purpose or an extravaganza or a satire was never clearly established at the time, but Maxim Gorki writing in the 'English Review' in 1924—when the shouting had died and the man who might have become the captain and the king of Irish drama had departed—gave this incisive summary of the "Playboy": "In it the comical side passes quite naturally into the terrible while the terrible becomes comical just as easily. J. M. Synge, like a truly wise artist, does not inject his own point of view; he just exhibits the people: they are half gods and half beasts, and are possessed of the childish desire to find a 'hero' among themselves."

Nothing so simple in the way of analysis would serve, however, in Dublin in 1907 where the real truth was that the Nationalists were not interested in artistic theories but only in what would advance their own hopes and longings. Therefore when Yeats conceived the truly democratic device of holding a public debate on the "Playboy" in the Abbey Theatre it was broken up in the same sort of disorder as had made some of the "Playboy" performances mere pantomine. But, before the cheers and the hisses and "A Nation Once Again" ended the affair, several strongly worded speeches had been made including one by a medical student, Mr. Sheehan, whose comments on Irishwomen and marriage and the survival of the fittest caused some disorder: "at this stage in the speech", one of the reporters reported, "many ladies whose countenances plainly indicated intense feelings of astonishment and pain, rose and left the place. Many men also retired."

It was at this point that "a young fellow from the stalls, under the influence of drink . . . ascended the stage and tried to speak but was removed" and the "debate" entered its last stages. Yeats gave his justification for the calling of the police and for his own action in making a charge against Mr. Beasley ("I did not want to charge a rowdy. I chose a man I could respect."). He was getting towards the end of a story about Edward Martyn, Lord Killanin and Mr. Arthur Symons and how they met an old fellow who hid for six months a man who had killed his father when "the meeting broke up with cheers, hisses and singing".

It was thought by Yeats, Lady Gregory and Synge that on the whole a famous victory had been won over the "Playboy". But Willie Fay was full of foreboding and pointed out that the public could always have the last word, especially in the country which invented the boycott. Something like a boycott followed, according to his recollection, and audiences were on the thin side though there was no doubt that the publicity over the "Playboy" affair had stirred up more general interest in the existence of the Abbey. Some of the business the Abbey might have gained from this, however, was being taken away by a new organisation, "The Theatre of Ireland" in which Maire nic Shiubhlaigh, who had never been particularly happy as a professional, took a leading part.

The productions for the rest of the year 1906 seemed to show a tendency towards playing safe, though they included probably the best of Lady Gregory's one-acters—"The Rising of the Moon"—which had enough patriotism in it to persuade some of the Nationalists that there might be hope of redemption for the Abbey if only the "British" or more accurately "West British" influence could be removed. But after things quietened down in relations between the Abbey and its audience they began promptly to bubble up again within the company.

The "new man" so long threatened had arrived. He was Ben Iden Payne who had been trained with Benson's company and who, after his few not particularly happy months at the Abbey, went on to become general manager to Miss Horniman's new venture, the Gaiety Theatre, Manchester. He married there one of the leading actresses, Mona Limerick, and their daughter, Rosalind Iden, is the wife of our only remaining actor-manager in England, Sir Donald Wolfit. Payne's background for the job in hand was impeccable. There were several ways in which he was infinitely more knowledgeable than the Fays, but he lacked whatever quality it was that made it possible for the Fays to get the best out of people who were either completely raw or only half-formed artistically. He put on a very successful production of Maeterlinck's "Interior" the first non-Irish play, except for Lady Gregory's translation of "Le Médecin malgré lui" that the Abbey had tackled. Payne's next production was "Fand", by Wilfrid Scawen Blunt, the first play by an Englishman, but on an Irish subject (and as an English poet Blunt devoted so much of his energies to denouncing British imperialism that the Nationalists almost felt him to be one of themselves). There was some question of producing "Oedipus Rex" with Payne playing the lead but Miss Horniman was against the idea on strictly practical grounds: "The point is this" she wrote to Yeats "I shall get the credit . . . of putting in an Englishman in Frank Fay's place, so as to spite Willie Fay. This would damage all concerned. It would cause friction and if Payne had to go a new man would be needed for America, if the company goes there. Could you not let Payne see that taking the part risks his post altogether?"

There was trouble too about a revival of "The King's Threshold". Willie Fay undertook the production, though his new contract had specified that he was to produce only dialect or "peasant" plays and was to have £100 a year extra for doing so. Miss Horniman regarded this as a breach of agreement and said so sharply. Indeed the tone of letters between Yeats and Miss Horniman was becoming sharper all the time: on the subject of some suggestion that she might like to mortgage the Abbey she wrote "you must understand my dear friend, that after your bringing that *impudent* message from Lady Gregory that I might mortgage the Abbey (you did not tell me *at the time* that it was her suggestion) that you have laid yourself open to be considered always by me as the messenger of the greed of the other directors and of Fay beyond them." And Yeats to Miss Horniman on a more trivial subject: "Your letter has made me extremely angry. If you had thought a moment you would have seen that the letter heading was a clerical error of Henderson or Payne's (I never saw it or heard of it till I got your letter) and yet you write a letter assuming that those you have been associated with for years are liars or rogues. It is intolerable." This was because Willie Fay's name had appeared on a newly-printed batch of writing paper as general manager instead of Payne's and Miss Horniman wrote to say that if this was the intention of the directors she would like to know so that she could cancel all arrangements about a new tour in Britain and also cancel both Payne's appointment and Willie Fay's extra £100 a year. She thought it would be as well, too, if somebody else were allowed to do new productions of Synge's plays and of Lady Gregory's. She may have withdrawn the extra £100 for Willie Fay, but a few weeks later she was still pumping money into the Abbey by sending £250 which was to be used for the forthcoming tour. She was alarmed by a proposal that the "Playboy" should not be played in London and said that she regarded this as a "political" decision. It was included in the tour and any attempts at demonstrations against it by Irish people in English cities petered out fairly quickly, though there was a warm reception for the play by some of the Liverpool Irish. Miss Horniman made no attempt to hide her dejection as it became clearer that her period of closely working with Yeats was at an end. "I am very anxious about your health" she wrote "and very sad that circumstances prevent me from being able to help to cure you. I would wish to clear away the difficulties which come between you and the quiet and leisure needed for the fine work we have a right to demand from you. That my scheme has hampered and hindered you instead of being a help is a sorrow to me." And later "I hope that when you have quite got rid of the remains of my old interference that you personally will see that I did my best to carry out the original scheme and that you will accept the fact that there is no place for you in it. Mr. Boyle would be much more useful, suitable and profitable in every way; if not Mr. Boyle, then some other man of like capacity. The very commonnesses in his work which you tried to get rid of are what are wanted, what are required in the natural development of a real theatre in Dublin for Dublin people. You and I tried to make it an Art theatre and we had not the living material to do it with. Your genius and my money together were helpless. We must both keep our promises uprightly, but we must not waste our gifts, we have no right to do so."

She gave a warning about the proposed American tour (which did not take place) that if it were run on "political" lines she would promptly withdraw her subsidy but added that if Irish-American sympathies could be aroused it would be possible to raise a large sum of money and "I could be bought out." She reckoned that it would cost £500 to pay her off for the remaining terms of the leases plus a fair valuation for the fittings of the theatre: yet she went on to inquire why nothing had been done about getting on with an extension to the backstage of the theatre which she would certainly have to pay for. She had calmed down considerably about the shortcomings, as she saw them, of the Fays; but that was only because her work was done in that direction. She was on the way out of the Abbey, but so were the Fays, Willie, Frank and Brigit (for Brigit O'Dempsey had married Willie Fay). It was a matter of only a very short time now before the final break came which had been building up for three years.

Chapter Nine

THE BREAK-UP

BEFORE the company left on its English tour the harm done by the "boycott" was showing itself plainly in the box-office returns. Eight performances brought in £158. In the previous few months £40 or £50 a night had been a fair average. Seven performances between April 1st and 6th produced only £30 although two of the plays were new ones—Winifred Letts's "The Eyes of the Blind" and "The Poorhouse" by Lady Gregory and Douglas Hyde. It was during these shows that Willie Fay used to invite the whole audience to come into the stalls to keep each other company. They sometimes filled no more than two rows.

But while the Dubliners stayed away, distinguished visitors from abroad became more frequent. J. M. Barrie, in Dublin for a production of "Peter Pan" was in the audience on the same night as Charles Frohman; Beerbohm Tree also saw some of the plays and Mrs. Patrick Campbell not only praised the players but said that she wanted to act in a play of Yeats's at the Abbey. Some years before she had shown an interest in "Diarmuid and Gráinne" sufficient to justify George Moore writing to Yeats: "I saw Mrs. Pat. She likes the play and would like to produce it. She even offers to pay a little on account. But she does not see her way to producing it in Dublin. . . . However her offer to pay money in advance convinces me that the play is good and it is a great thing to know that." Perhaps Moore did not know that Mrs. Pat had also commented to Yeats about the play "Oh Mr. Yeats, what a pity you did not write it all yourself". But she showed some wisdom in not wanting to play it

in Dublin—more wisdom, indeed, than those who entrusted
it to F. R. Benson and his company; but that was well in the
past and the production of "Diarmuid and Gráinne" at least
has this place in Irish theatre history—that it was the last time
Dubliners had to call in English actors before they could see a
production of an Irish play.

The visit of Frohman, a famous and prosperous American
theatrical producer who was also branching out in London
caused a curious rumour to circulate which was quickly denied
by Miss Horniman. It was to the effect that Frohman was trying
to buy the Abbey and take over the management, and that he
was on the way to succeeding. He said himself, when somebody
thought of tracing the rumour back to its possible source that
no such idea had ever occurred to him. He could only suppose
it arose because the fact of his being in Dublin had been so
heavily reported in the Irish newspapers. He was there because
wherever an interesting theatre was to be seen Frohman liked
to turn up. But although he might not have known it then
Frohman was to enter very much into the history of the Abbey
before many months went by.

Payne's sudden decision to resign and not to return to Dublin
after the tour must have been a particularly hard blow to Miss
Horniman. For the second time, after long campaigning she
had had her way and it had failed. The first was over the im-
portation of Miss Darragh from London to displace Sarah Allgood
from the leading parts in Yeats plays. Miss Darragh had a feeling
for Irish legend but was entirely London trained and her appearance in 1906 as Deirdre had proved Miss Horniman's theory
about imposing English standards on the Abbey to be quite
wrong. Miss Darragh's performances were successful and much
applauded, but as Willie Fay said, it was like putting a Rolls
Royce to run in a race with a lot of hill ponies up the mountains
of Mourne. The ponies could outpace the Rolls all the way;
though they were less of a mechanical marvel they had natural
advantages. So, although she was so much more accomplished
Miss Darragh was made to appear stilted. Her engagement
quickly ended, to Miss Horniman's great disappointment.
And here was another of her nominees, Payne, discovering in
a very short time indeed that he could not find a way of working

with the Abbey company which would combine the normal procedure of the English repertory theatre with the methods which had been worked out by the Fays and their colleagues for running a repertory theatre, Dublin style.

Willie Fay had to be reinstated in full after Payne left but he felt that his authority had been weakened and that there would have to be a serious attempt to impose some real professional discipline on the company.

He made five proposals in a letter dated December 1st, 1907. They were:

1. That the Directors put up a notice shortly that all contracts with the National Theatre Society terminate on such a day. That people wishing to re-engage write in to W. G. Fay.

2. That all engagements be for a season only and terminable by a fortnight's notice on either side.

3. That where the Directors require special actors or actresses for their performances I should engage them on terms to be decided between the Directors and myself and for such parts or performances as the Directors shall decide.

4. That the power of dismissing those under my contracts shall rest with me after due consultation with the Directors in the case of principals.

5. That there shall be no appeal to any other authority than mine by the people engaged by me on all matters dealt with in their contracts.

The five points could all be reduced to a single one: that Willie Fay should be given complete authority over the company, as he might expect to have in a well-organised theatre. The indiscipline he complained of had shown itself on tour and during preparation for new productions. Willie Fay had reported to Yeats that Sarah Allgood and Maire O'Neill persistently missed rehearsals. He complained further that as he had no direct control over them and no power to make them obey his orders he must refuse to accept any responsibility about the date of productions arranged. "My agreement with the Directors" he wrote to Yeats "on taking over the management of this theatre again, at a reduced salary, was that there was to be no communication between any of the employees of the theatre and the Directors except through me as Manager . . . the company think that if they dont like to obey my orders, they can appeal to the Directors. If you and Mr. Synge have a plan for getting into better working order here, the sooner it is put into operation the better."

In an agreement dated 15th February, 1907, signed by W. B. Yeats and William G. Fay there is no clause about communication through the Manager, so he presumably referred to a later one which I have not seen. But the directors did not agree that the company had ever lost the right of appeal, as their reply to Willie Fay's five points shows. There was a Directors' meeting on December 4th to consider his letter and the decisions were:

1. That we could not agree to his proposal about dismissal of the Company and re-engagement by him personally.

2. That we cannot enlarge the powers already given under contract.

3. We cannot abrogate the right of appeal to the Directors already possessed by the Company.

4. That an improvement in discipline is necessary, and that rules with this object be drawn up in consultation with the Company. That the Company be asked to elect, say, three members to consult with the Stage Manager and Directors as to the rules of discipline. That the rules so drawn up be put to the company as a whole for their decision.

5. That it be explained to the Company that this Theatre must go on as a theatre for intellectual drama, whatever unpopularity that may involve. That no compromise can be accepted on this subject, but that if any member find himself unable to go on with us under the circumstances, we will not look upon it as unfriendly on his part if he go elsewhere, on the contrary we will help him all we can.

6. That henceforth a Director must always go with the Company upon the more important tours.

It seems clear that the Directors did not envisage the departure of the Fays as a result of this turning down of Willie's five points.

When they did decide to "go elsewhere" they got no help whatever from the directorate—quite the contrary.

Before the Directors' meeting Yeats and Synge had been thinking deeply about reorganisation. Yeats produced a very long memorandum on the subject, a rambling document, but with a lot of commonsense in it and some very frank assessments of the Company. In the preamble he made the important point that "At the present moment the theatre is extremely accomplished in the performance of Irish peasant comedy and in nothing else. It cannot run indefinitely on peasant comedy for to do that will be to tire its audiences out and come to an end for lack of plays. The popularity of the Theatre at this moment depends upon two writers, Mr. Boyle and Lady Gregory; I do not say that individual plays by other writers have not assisted them but these are the only two writers who can be counted upon to draw audiences . . . my work will hardly draw large audiences for a considerable time, and though verse drama might well create a school of very varied temperament there is certainly no sign of another verse dramatist."

He reasoned that the Abbey would multiply its chances of creating writers if it widened its capacity for performance and he thought the natural way to do this was to perform "selections from foreign masterpieces chosen as much for a means of training as for anything else." He restated the final object of the Abbey as the creation of a National Theatre something after the Continental pattern—though it had been fairly clear in the early stages that what the Fays and their early collaborators were after was a National Theatre on a purely Irish pattern. Yeats thought the theatre should be capable of showing its audience examples of all great schools of drama and believed that "to be artistically noble it will have to be the acknowledged centre for some kind of art which no other Theatre in the world has in the same perfection." (This was what some critics, especially in England, believed to be precisely the unique virtue of the Abbey up to then.) Coming to the immediate future he concluded that at the moment the executive side of the theatre depended on one overworked man and upon a group of players who were necessarily chosen for highly specialised work. Therefore other "forms of personality and activity" would have to be added.

I

The natural course was to find more capital and engage some
actor or actors whose imaginations "will express themselves in
other forms of work with the same ease and abundance with
which Mr. Fay's imagination expresses itself in comedy. He is
not a romantic actor, he is not a tragic actor, he is a very clever
man and can do not badly many things that are not his natural
work". But he thought an entirely different kind of man needed
to be found with the financial help of a hypothetical businessman,
or even of Miss Horniman (which seemed overoptimistic). The
new backer would be told that the existing company knew
all about Irish comedy and could have no interference there
and that "Mr. Yeats must of course retain the rights natural to
the only verse writer in the Theatre. . . ." Otherwise they would
be ready to employ any efficient professional help, including
teachers, that could be found by showing a willingness to pay
for it.

Yeats foresaw that Willie Fay and the hypothetical man would
work in complete freedom and amity because they would be
doing different things and the theatre would be playing continuously. Still harping on Miss Horniman, he speculated about
whether she might be willing to supply the necessary capital and
thought that if so she might engage some old actor ("if Herman
Vezin were a little younger he would serve her turn") and put
him in charge of the non-Irish work. "It is hardly necessary
to add that such a theatre would probably require a paid managing director to correlate all its activities. It would be expensive
but not too expensive if Miss Horniman desired it and if our own
audiences go on improving for a little while. I do not however
think that Miss Horniman would be ready for a scheme of this
kind at the present moment. I can see William Fay's face as he
reads this sentence. It will brighten like the face of a certain old
Fenian when Mrs. MacBride's Italian revolutionist wound
up a detailed project for a rising in Connacht with the sentence
'I see no chance of success. . . .' "

He then changed to a more directly practical theme by ad-
mitting that the larger scheme was impossible for the moment,
and that a smaller one would have to be regarded as urgent.
"William Fay must be freed from all work except his artistic
work so that the comedies may be as fine as possible . . . instead

of enlarging our work which we cannot do without capital we must perfect what we have and that is principally comedy. . . . We must see that William Fay's own work, which should be the chief attraction of all our comedies, is given the opportunity to develop". He showed some concern about what would happen if Willie Fay were too grossly overworked; he might become monotonous in his acting, he might be satisfied to express his own personality instead of creating new characters. So the business and non-artistic side of the theatre should be given to somebody else to ensure that the chief comedian did not become inefficient. Yeats also felt that measures could be taken towards greater efficiency in other sides of the Abbey's work. Frank Fay, for instance, he regarded as "a born teacher of elocution up to a certain point . . . people come from his hands certainly with great clearness of elocution, with a fine feeling for both line and passage as units of sound, with a sufficient though less infallible sense of accent, but without passion, without expression, either in voice or gesture." Lapsing into the past tense he recalled that Maire Walker (Maire nic Shiubhlaigh) had no passion or power of characterisation in verse, but considerable and rather delicate expressiveness, that Miss Garvey (Mrs. George Roberts) was a verse speaker of more feeling, even with some slight touch of passion, though a very narrow range; and that he did not regret Starkey "though he could get through a quiet passage creditably."

Frank Fay, Yeats thought, was "always beautiful to listen to, but he is not improving; I am not quite sure that he is as good as he was." On the women he brought himself to say something which discretion must often have hinted was better left unsaid. "From the first day of the Theatre I have known that it is almost impossible for us to find a passionate woman actress in Catholic Ireland . . . I must therefore have the right to bring in a player or players from without when I can do so without burdening the finances of the company more than my work is worth." He ended his long memorandum by suggesting that no great changes were required immediately except that the non-artistic work should be taken off Willie Fay's shoulders and Miss Darragh or Mrs. Emery (Florence Farr) should be brought in occasionally to play in some foreign masterpiece.

It was all carefully thought out and much of it was perfectly reasonable. But it came too late. As soon as he got the Directors' reply to his five points Willie Fay wrote out his resignation. His wife (Brigit O'Dempsey) and his brother Fank Fay did not hesitate a moment; they joined him and the Abbey Theatre which had owed so much of its early success to the Fays lost them and became once again the centre of a major controversy.

The clamour and excitement about the Fays leaving the Abbey was almost as great as the noise about the "Playboy". It was, in fact, a more serious matter because even allowing for the effects of the partial boycott the theatre was finding it easy to recover from the "Playboy" business. Would it be able to get over the departure of the Fays?

The newspapers were full of leading articles, interviews, letters all giving conflicting opinions and contradictory information about the causes of the breach and its possible cure. There was a strong tendency to put the whole of the blame on Yeats. By my reading of the correspondence, some of which I have quoted, this was unjust, or at least only flimsily justifiable. The reasons for the clash were as clear as they possibly could be to those directly concerned yet both the contending sides allowed explanations to be given which were far from the facts. So far from the facts, indeed, that one theory seriously put forward was that "internal dissensions produced by the staging of the 'Playboy' have at length developed into what is described as mutiny among the principal members of the histrionic company."

The confusion was added to by Yeats sending out to the press in advance a paragraph he had written for the forthcoming "Samhain" saying that ". . . it is sufficient to show the spirit in which we part." It read: "We are about to lose our principal actor. William Fay has had enough of it and we don't wonder, and he is going to some other country where his exquisite gift of comedy and his brain teeming with fancy will bring him an audience, fame, and a little money. He has worked with us now since 1902, when he formed his company to carry on the work of the Irish Literary Theatre, and feels that he must leave to the younger men the long, laborious battle. We have his good wishes and he will return to us if at all possible to play his old parts for some brief season or seasons and may possibly rejoin us for a

London or an American tour. We believe that William Fay is right to go and he will have our good will and good wishes with him though we have lost, in losing him, the finest comedian of his kind upon the English-speaking stage."

This was misleading in at least two ways. There had never been a question of Willie Fay's wanting to leave to earn more money. He had only a few days before the Directors' meeting pointed out that for his latest contract he accepted less salary than before. As he was well under 40 and a demon for work the suggestion that he wanted to leave the battle to younger men was meaningless. He was such an energetic man, with such staying power that in spite of Miss Horniman's jibe about his disliking the hard working professional life he was still at it on the stage and in the film studios twenty years after Miss Horniman had thrown in her hand altogether, seen her beloved Gaiety in Manchester become a cinema, and retired from the theatre completely. In spite of its warm compliments the "Samhain" paragraph contained such inaccuracies that it is hard to see why Willie Fay agreed to its publication.

The confusion was not lessened by Frank Fay who gave an interview at the quayside before leaving to join his brother in London where they were to prepare for their American tour under Frohman's management. He said he was leaving Ireland with a certain amount of regret but that he had no complaint to make about the Abbey Theatre. He said that the parting was caused by ". . . a friendly difference of opinion on certain matters already published, and instead of feeling any ill-will against the institution he wished it every success." In particular he was at pains to point out that the Fays had not been lured away from Dublin by "Mr. Frohman's Gold."

One thing was clear in all this confusion. If the rest of the company knew just what the row was about they kept remarkably quiet, and that was uncharacteristic as anybody will realise who knows how actors and actresses talk.

They knew remarkably little about the inside story and this seems well borne out by the fact that in May, 1908, four months after the Fays had gone, four of them said so publicly. They had read an account of an interview in a Chicago paper giving Willie Fay's reasons for leaving—or rather giving the reasons as he then preferred to describe them. Yeats sent a short letter to a Dublin paper giving the gist of Willie Fay's suggestions about reorganisation and of the Directors' refusal. This was followed immediately by a letter to the Editor.

"Sir, with reference to the statements made by Mr. W. G. Fay in the 'Chicago Sunday Tribune' . . . the directors have for the first time acquainted us with the true facts concerning the resignation of Mr. W. G. Fay, and allowed us to see the proposals made by him on the occasion. The acceptance of the proposals of Mr. W. G. Fay by the directors would have led to the dissolution of the company, and we, the undersigned, take this opportunity to say that we certainly would not have rejoined under Mr. Fay's proposed conditions.

Signed {
Sarah Allgood
Arthur Sinclair
J. M. Kerrigan
Maire O'Neill
}

If I had finished my explorations among the mountains of Abbey letters and documents while Willie Fay was still alive there are many questions I should like to have asked him. Having consented (at least by silence) to Yeats's putting out a misleading version of his reasons for resigning why did he later put out a different reason himself? It was not long before he was explaining that one of the reasons for the quarrel was that the directors failed to put on new plays by unknown authors. Did Frank Fay know every detail of his brothers' management troubles? It seems inconceivable that he did not, so he must have supported the policy of concealing the true reason for the Fays' departure. When he sent long personal letters to his friend W. J. Lawrence, who was certainly in his confidence, Frank Fay never referred to the question of his brother's difficulties as stage manager. He frequently repeated the point about the number of plays by Yeats and Lady Gregory and seemed to take it for granted that it was these two who were principally responsible for the final upheaval. Synge he rarely mentioned except as keeping in the background "for reasons of his own".

Neither brother ever uttered a hint of criticism against Miss Horniman, the strongest of the many missing links in the whole story. Why not?

It seems to me the only possible explanation is that they had no idea what was going on behind their backs. One point that could be cleared up only by somebody who took part in the argument (and they are all dead) is whether the directors really believed that Willie Fay insisted on the right to engage the players so that they were under contract to him personally. He asserted many a time that this was not his intention and that he had never allowed anybody to think he intended it. When he spoke of "people wishing to re-engage to write in to W. G. Fay" and of "people engaged by me" he was referring to what he believed the minimum of managerial authority, the right to hire and fire and to have proper understandings about how much notice was to be given on either side. As hirer and firer he would, of course, have been acting on behalf of the directors. Either he failed to make himself clear on this most important principle, or the directors preferred not to understand him.

Whatever the obscurities about why the Fays left, and whether or not some of them were deliberately created, all pretence of a "friendly difference" soon disappeared and there was open war between the Abbey and the Fays who had done so much to create it.

Writing from New York on February 19th, 1908, to W. J. Lawrence, Frank Fay complained: "We are described on the advertising bills as 'The Irish National Theatre Co. from Dublin' . . . and they have used Yeats's name to boom the thing, all I needn't say against my wishes, but one can't interfere". He added that "one of the papers let the cat out of the bag about our having left the Abbey Theatre". Yeats's father, his sister and his close friend John Quinn (who also acted as his agent) were in New York at the time and none of them called on the Fays until Quinn turned up. He complained of the advertisements (which had been written by Frohman's office) and demanded that the name "Irish National Theatre Co." should be removed. There was no reason to refuse this and Willie Fay asked several times that it should be done, but the Frohman office evidently thought the whole thing a fuss about nothing and did not make any changes in the publicity. Quinn then threatened to seek an injunction to stop further performances. After more wrangling and more threats the company was advertised as "The Irish Players from Dublin, Ireland"—a name which was adopted and successfully used in later years by companies of Abbey players.

The gloves were off in Dublin too, and there was no more pretence. After they had been threatened with legal action in New York the Fays heard that a special meeting of the Society had suspended them from membership. This was done under a rule which forbade members "taking part in any performances other than those given by the Society" without giving notice and receiving permission. "Your breach of this rule," Synge wrote, as secretary of the Society, "might in different circumstances have been merely technical but recent misunderstandings and misrepresentation have made this step necessary in the interests of the Society."

The wheel had certainly turned full circle when the two men who, as Yeats said time after time, made the Abbey Theatre a possibility were themselves repudiated by the Society and expelled. They felt bitter about it and their bitterness was increased by the fact that they thought Yeats and Lady Gregory were both demanding extortionate payments for the use of their plays in America. Lady Gregory apparently realised that her agent had gone too far and, according to Frank "wrote to my brother returning half the royalties and saying she'd 'give a good deal more if she could undo the trouble of the last few months'; (which she is largely responsible for) but my brother has of course returned the cheque."

Although they were in good acting form and (with Brigit O'Dempsey, Dudley Digges and J. M. Kerrigan) offered New York as strong a team as could be found at the time in Dublin, the company did not go down well. Frank Fay was not a bit surprised for he had already come to quite downright conclusions about Americans: "Irish life they neither understand nor desire to understand; Why should they? It means failure and they worship success. The 'Rising' goes better than 'The Pot' but the principal critic here, Alan Dale, told the critic of the 'World' (Mr. Darnton) that there was nothing to write about. I'm afraid some of our great dramatists will get the conceit taken out of them if they come here."

Whether or not the Irish players were ready to face American audiences it was clear that the audiences had not yet come to appreciate either the plays or the acting as warmly as they did some years later. The Fays were neither a great success nor a miserable failure and when the full Abbey company followed them three years later they had a very mixed reception indeed—even to the point of the whole company being hauled up in a police court for performing an "immoral or indecent play" by name "The Playboy of the Western World".

There is a very bitter note in Frank Fay's letters to Lawrence and he harps constantly on dishonest and crooked treatment meted out by Yeats. Yet within two years he was longing to get back to Dublin and was writing both to Yeats and Lady Gregory offering to come back to the Abbey and modestly guessing that he might be worth £2 a week.

It was ten years later before he appeared at the Abbey again and then only in very occasional revivals of "The Hour Glass" or "The King's Threshold". Willie Fay never again played at the Abbey and rarely visited Dublin at all. The end of the story was a dismal one with recriminations flying both ways and generosity out of the question.

Yet the theatre was well enough established to avoid the disaster which some people forecast so confidently. It did not collapse when the Fays left, partly because by that time the company—largely trained by them— was strong enough to survive without its leading comedian and chief verse speaker. Sarah Allgood was developing fast and there were Arthur Sinclair, Maire O'Neill and J. M. Kerrigan at hand to support her. It was also necessary to make up for the absence of Brigit O'Dempsey who had been building up a strong position and would presumably have become one of the leading actresses if she had not left with her husband.

There was also a period of good fortune with dramatists. A new one, who then called himself S. L. Robinson, turned up in 1909 and has never left the Abbey since. As producer, manager, author and director Lennox Robinson became the "father" of the Abbey Theatre and built a record of service and devotion which nobody has bettered. Another playwright who arrived just before Robinson was W. F. Casey who wrote two successful plays and seemed likely to become one of the regular dramatists—but he went off to London and became editor of the "Times". He also acted as secretary of the Society for a time and has good stories to tell of the ingenuous way the theatre was run even four years after it opened. One of his best illustrates the alleged unworldliness of Yeats for when Casey presented at the bank certain cheques for salaries and other expenses the cashier brought them back, puzzled, to enquire "Mr. Casey: why does your director sign his cheques 'yours sincerely, W. B. Yeats'?"

T. C. Murray arrived after Casey had gone and the corps of playwrights continued to renew itself while the acting strength of the company increased. A burst of publicity almost equal to those caused by the "Playboy" and the departure of the Fays followed the decision to produce Shaw's "The Shewing-up of Blanco Posnet". This had been unaccountably banned by the Lord Chamberlain for British production and the Abbey proposed to exploit the fact that there was no theatre censorship in Ireland (there still is none) and put the play on for the first time in the United Kingdom. The authorities at Dublin Castle were annoyed and rumbled threats, but they had no legal basis and the play was successfully presented.

In spite of these various good fortunes, though, the Abbey still had its troubles with Miss Horniman. Her disengagement was planned and had begun before the Fays left but it was not to be carried out without more bickering. She was asking very little of the directors but it took a long exchange of letters to bring about the transfer of the Abbey and even then it was not done until the lawyers had had a hand in it, an arbitrator had been appointed (Mr. C. P. Scott, Editor of the "Manchester Guardian") and his arbitration wasted because Miss Horniman argued with its terms.

It was a sordid ending to what had been a noble partnership and the break-up was not without a personal side. In one of the early financial arguments (at the end of 1909) about the exact cost of the theatre Miss Horniman wrote to Yeats ". . . Even Super People cannot be expected to enjoy a revolt of slaves, but I have been driven to this. I suffered very acutely at first when you changed in your attitude towards me; gradually, very gradually, it is true, after your return from America. I fought against this by trying to ignore your unkindness, but strive as I might it grew and grew . . . Yours, Annie."

The argument on which Mr. Scott was asked to arbitrate was based on Miss Horniman's anger at the fact that the Abbey Theatre was opened on the night of King Edward VII's funeral. Lady Gregory had advised Lennox Robinson to close but the telegram arrived too late (which cost a telegraph boy his job). Miss Horniman regarded this as a "political" gesture and refused to pay two instalments of her subsidy. C. P. Scott found against her, saying that she "was and is not justified in refusing to pay the two instalments . . . on First June and First September, 1910."

Miss Horniman's solicitors wrote offering to "settle the matter at any time on receiving a statement showing the adjustments that have to be made." But they added "Our client wishes us to make it clear that if this money is paid it is solely because she accepts the Arbitrator's award, and that she still holds that there was an agreement as to 'no politics', that the agreement was broken, and that she should not have been called upon to pay the money. We cannot help thinking that Miss Horniman is being very badly used." On the same date Yeats and Lady Gregory wrote to Miss Horniman saying "We have just had Mr. Scott's award. We wish at once to say that remembering all your generosity in the past it was never our intention to press the legal point against you. If with all the facts before you you still cannot accept the integrity of our action, we cannot accept the money and the matter is at an end." This was confirmed by a solicitor's letter; Yeats thanked Scott for his help and Scott replied "I'm glad if you think some good at least has been done. I was interested in the work and it was a gain anyway to be made acquainted with yourself and Lady Gregory."

In this sour atmosphere Miss Horniman's connection with the Abbey theatre was brought to an end; she remained generous to the last and the terms of transfer amounted to her virtually giving the theatre to the Society free. She had spent not less than £12,000 and possibly as much as £15,000 on the property, including subsidies and covering the losses on some tours. She asked only for £1,428 to cover what she paid for the various

leases and it was for this sum, or possibly even less, that the
Abbey Theatre, fully equipped and with an expanding audience
became the sole property of the National Theatre Society. Even
this was not done without some unpleasantness and in January
1911 Miss Horniman was threatening legal proceedings against
the Directors for non payment of £1,000 due to her and ending
her letter ". . . unless I am paid there will be a scandal of the
Directors' own making which will damage the future of the
Abbey." The necessary payments were made and Miss Horniman
disappeared entirely from the Irish scene.

Chapter Ten

PAST, PRESENT AND FUTURE

THE midwife was dismissed; the birth of the Abbey theatre was successfully completed. It came noisily into the world, had its childish illnesses but grew up sturdy.

Certainly the first aim of the Irish National Theatre Society was fully realised. Whatever troubles it had in the early years and later on, the Abbey did become Ireland's National Theatre in the fullest sense especially when, after a dozen unsubsidised years, Miss Horniman as patroness was replaced by the government of the Irish Free State which started by putting up £850 a year and has extended its subsidy from time to time until it now stands at £8,000 a year plus £3,000 for encouraging plays in Irish. In 1957-58 the sum made available was £34,000 which includes a first grant toward re-building the burnt-out Abbey.

It did not become the Gaelic speaking national theatre that Frank Fay originally said was the only possible national theatre for Ireland. Irish speaking actors and actresses are now almost a hundred per cent. of the company and the ability to act in Irish as well as English is required of all aspirants to the company nowadays. Yet in twelve years from 1938 to 1950 only forty Irish plays were staged. While the revival of the Irish language remains government policy the Abbey Theatre will have to continue trying to do two different and in some ways contradictory tasks and many of its present-day critics believe this is responsible for a decline in its standards. But the supporters of the compulsory Irish policy both in education and in the theatre itself are convinced that it will work. They insist that there is now a Dublin audience for plays in Irish which can enjoy them as much as if they were in English. But the only really popular pieces the

Abbey has put on in Irish are Christmas shows based on the English pantomime tradition. If there is an audience for Irish plays it keeps itself to itself though it is given preferential treatment by the directorate of the Abbey which keeps on building up its Irish-speaking company for the sake of a mere half dozen plays or so each year. The supporters and detractors of the Irish policy will never agree; on the one side they say that it is destroying the theatre and lowering the standards of acting. On the other they assert that it has strenghtened the company, magnified the importance of the drama in Irish culture and that it holds great hopes and prospects for the future.

Whatever its troubles in the early years and later on, and whatever the outcome may be of the Gaelicisation, the Abbey has become one of the leading theatres of the world and an attraction for foreign visitors in Dublin. Its influence on acting technique is nothing like that of the Moscow Art Theatre, its style of acting (at any rate in English) has not become accepted as a national pattern as with the Théâtre Français, but it gave a lead to the "little theatre" in Britain and even more in the United States. It gave Miss Horniman both the inspiration and the experience she needed to become, on the management side, the most important woman in the history of the theatre in Britain. A possible exception was Lilian Baylis, who herself acknowledged that it was Miss Horniman's Gaiety Theatre in Manchester which showed her the way she wanted to build up the Old Vic in London although its line of development has been strictly that of a Shakespearean rather than of a general repertory theatre. It is possible, through these two great women to trace a direct link between the ideas and motives behind the Abbey Theatre and the Old Vic which is now officially embodied in the English National Theatre committee and as plans now run will be the company to occupy the British national theatre if it is ever built.

The world owes Dublin something for setting a pattern for much of the theatre organisation in this century in the English-speaking countries and that is a great contribution; but it is only part of what the Abbey has sent out to the world. It sent its dramatists—Yeats, Lady Gregory, Synge, Colum, Lennox Robinson, St. John Ervine, Sean O'Casey to be performed all over the world in English or translated into a dozen languages. Some of the plays have not transplanted well and it is still something of an ordeal to see English or American companies attempting Synge or O'Casey who got the essence of their countrymen so completely into dramatic form that they deprived their work of complete universality. An English Pegeen Mike or a Swedish Joxer Daly can never quite bring off what the authors demanded but this does not discourage them from trying. The Abbey style transplants well to the United States. I have seen in Boston a Paul Vincent Carroll play, "The Wayward Saint" being tried out on the way to Broadway (where it failed) and the production might have been designed for the Abbey and played by the Dublin company. In fact only two or three of the cast were from the Abbey but the rest of them had sufficient of the authentic style to make an Abbey play of something which had not, up to that time, been staged at all in Ireland.

Abbey actors and actresses have become as well known in London, New York and Hollywood as they ever were at home and are so much better rewarded there that it has become difficult to keep the best of them in Dublin. The salaries have gone up a lot since Willie Fay was paid £4 a week and Frank Fay £2 but they have not kept pace with theatre salaries elsewhere and it has become distressingly true that some of Ireland's best actors now say they cannot afford to play in the Abbey company. F. J. McCormick, who was paid hundreds of pounds a week for making a film like "Odd Man Out" never earned more than £14 a week as the chief actor of the Abbey and there are members of the company now whose salaries would not keep them if they were not able to pick up a little extra by broadcasting or by television. Lady Gregory once spoke of an actress needing an extra few shillings a week "because she has a husband and children to keep" but on present theatrical salaries in Dublin family life must be very difficult indeed.

The financial background of the theatre has, of course, been built up on the tiny auditorium of the Abbey itself rather than on the more normal sized one of the Queen's Theatre where the Abbey company continues to play. This limitation on the audience has long been a drag and as long ago as 1915 St. John Ervine was rebuked by Lady Gregory for having "seven-leagued ideas" because he wanted to found a touring company to cover Cork, Belfast, Londonderry, Galway, Wexford and other Irish towns without having to close down the Abbey in Dublin. It was not a good theatre for letting to other companies because of its size so that when the permanent company went on tour the Abbey lay empty, consuming overheads and producing no profit. Ervine thought he saw a gleam of hope during the 1916 rebellion in Dublin. He thought the Abbey might be shelled or burned and that the compensation money would build a theatre more suitable for operation. "But" he wrote twenty years later "when, at last the Rebellion was quelled and I went down to Marlborough Street in high hope, what did I find? Houses on the other side of the street were level with the ground, mere heaps of hot ash but not a pane of glass in the Abbey was broken. I cursed the Government and the crew of the Helga for their incompetence, and bitterly regretted that I had not gone down on Easter Monday and fired it myself." Ervine was not to be given the chance of remodelling the theatre. Politics drove him out of Dublin and deprived the Abbey of a man who might have done great things for it. But Lady Gregory and Lennox Robinson pulled the Abbey through some very hard times and stubbornly kept to the objective of running a theatre on lines which any commercial manager would say led straight to bankruptcy. Sometimes it very nearly did, but the theatre gained enormously from being outside the framework of the ordinary commercial theatre.

It had begun at a time when Henry Irving was at the end of his career but Ellen Terry, Sir George Alexander and Beerbohm Tree were at their full power, when Bernhardt and Duse were at their height, when the youngsters learning their trade included Henry Ainley, Harcourt Williams, Matheson Lang and Oscar Asche, when Shaw and Wilde and Pinero were dazzling the great world. The theatre was still the chief form of public entertainment without the many kinds of competition it has today and the commercial theatre offered an actor a steady living. The roguery and vagabondage of the stage were just merging into a more respectable Bohemianism. The Shavian revolution had not swept through the English theatre to bring with it the demand for the "intellectual" actor and actress. There were no repertory theatres in Liverpool, Manchester, Birmingham, Glasgow when the Abbey began. So it had to create its own methods in every department for it had no model to copy from. Such attempts as were made to fit it into the commercial mould failed and it was almost entirely by a trial and error process that methods of managing the Abbey were discovered and developed. It was always open to more outside influences than any normal theatre would be. The Playboy riots and the boycott that followed them were one form. There was another form of it from viceregal society which gradually gathered that although Lady Gregory, Miss Horniman and Mr. Yeats were gentlefolk there was something highly suspicious about a company which put on allegories about Irish independence and never played "God Save the King" after its performances. There was Dublin Castle displeasure about "Blanco Posnet", I.R.A. pressure in 1921 when the theatre was ordered to close for a period of "national mourning" but all these were courageously and stubbornly resisted. The one which did succeed was that applied to make it more an Irish speaking theatre. This became the main mission in life of Mr. Ernest Blythe first as a director, then as managing director. As this pressure came from within it had more success.

There were more benign pressures, too, as the Abbey consolidated itself and began to move out of the first stage of its life. Ireland was not going to be content indefinitely with the drama as conceived by Yeats, in which poetry was the mainspring, or even as conceived by Synge to whom peasant life could be exploited to say things about the world which were far beyond peasant philosophy. Realism was the word abroad and realism had to come to the Irish theatre—not the Zola form of realism with which George Moore flirted, but an exhilarating Irish form of it brought to the Abbey by Lennox Robinson and T. C. Murray, the forerunners of the "Cork Realists". They dealt with everyday life and problems and were not committed in advance to the romantic or mystical view as taken by Yeats. A flavour of Ulster sharpness was introduced by George Shiels, who wrote regularly for twenty five years from 1921. A play of his established the first record for a long run

K

at the Abbey—three months of "The Rugged Path". The path was leading away from Yeats's belief:

> "John Synge, I and Augusta Gregory, thought
> All that we did, all that we said or sang
> Must come from contact with the soil, from that
> Contact everything Antaeus-like grew strong."

It led to Sean O'Casey whose appearance could not even have been guessed at in the wildest dreams of anybody who was in at the beginning of the Irish theatre movement. His coming meant virtually the end of Yeats as anything more than a traditional antiquity to be revived in a reverent spirit from time to time on special occasions. I cannot agree with Eric Bentley that "theatre people outside Dublin have never heard of him" but I can endorse his further statement that "Even in Dublin his plays were never the favourites and by now most of them have disappeared from the Abbey Theatre's repertoire". The disappearance was hastened by O'Casey's eruption on to the Abbey stage. His dealings with the theatre began, as they ended, with the rejection of a play. He did not at all fit in with any of the Abbey pre-conceptions and it is as well that Miss Horniman was well out of the way when he arrived for he was not only an unskilled labourer but a fanatic for the Irish language, a trade union organiser and secretary of the Irish Citizen Army. He left the Citizen Army before 1916 but his first book was a short history of its appearance and disappearance on the Irish political scene. His first play, "Frost in the Flower" and another one "The Crimson in the Tricolour" were rejected by the Abbey and perhaps it was this which made him decide that he had better study the sort of work they accepted. His theatregoing had been done at the Queen's before this but he paid three or four visits to the Abbey before getting down to serious work on "The Shadow of a Gunman".

I readily admit to a prejudice about Sean O'Casey. I believe him to be one of the world's great dramatists, one of the greatest writers Ireland has ever produced. I have criticised his work at times for its political slant and its trend towards shapelessness. One of my bitterest disappointments in the Dublin theatre was watching "The Bishop's Bonfire" and believing in the first act that O'Casey had brought off what might be his best play. The sag in the second act and the evaporation of all drama in the third were dreadful to see.

But he wrote other plays before that one and, much as it may seem sometimes to displease him, the theatre of the world insists on regarding "Juno and the Paycock", "The Shadow of a Gunman" and "The Plough and the Stars" as his masterpieces. "Juno" has even survived being truncated to make a television play at which English critics sniped because it under-emphasised the comedy, although the play is crystal clearly a tragedy in which the principal theme is expressed in the words "Sacred Heart of Jesus, take away our hearts o' stone, and give us hearts o' flesh! Take away this murdherin' hate, an' give us Thine own eternal love!"

When those words were first heard from the stage at the Abbey a tremor ran through the audience unlike anything felt since the first works of Synge had burst upon Dublin. The Abbey audience reserved its highest compliment for O'Casey. It booed, hissed and protested at his "The Plough and the Stars" when it was first produced in 1926. Since his theme was the freedom of Ireland, his very title taken from the banners of the Citizen Army, O'Casey was reluctant to have the police called. But they were called, after the audience had overflowed from the stalls on to the stage itself to argue with the actors.

The shouting sounded very much like what had been heard during the "Playboy"—"an insult to Irish womanhood," "a slander against the good name of the Citizen Army." There were two crucial differences. It was Yeats himself who sent for the police and this time they were not employees of a British government but Ireland's own constabulary: they stopped the row pretty quickly with decisive action, leaving comparative peace behind as they took out the noisiest demonstrators; and leaving Yeats on the stage raging at the ignorance of the audience he had spent quarter of a century trying to educate. "I thought you had got tired of this . . . You have disgraced yourselves again. Is this to be an ever-recurring celebration of the arrival of Irish genius? Once more you have rocked the cradle of genius. The news of what is happening here will go from country to country. You have once more rocked the cradle of reputation. The fame of O'Casey is born tonight. This is his apotheosis."

Two years after this when the cradle of genius had a new child of O'Casey's in it, "The Silver Tassie", his brief, glorious career as an Abbey playwright ceased. After deep consideration and interminable correspondence the directors refused the play, and their ban remained in force for nine years. This not only generated a row of true Abbey proportions but it so incensed O'Casey that he refused to meet Lady Gregory in London later the same year, when the play was being produced there and ran for eight weeks. "The production" he wrote to Lady Gregory, "has made my mind a flood again of thoughts about the play's rejection by the Abbey Directors, and bitterness would certainly enter into things I would say about W. B. Yeats and L. Robinson, if we were to meet, bitterness that would hurt you, and I am determined to avoid hurting you as much as possible."

What if he had never quarrelled? Would he have brought the Abbey Theatre with its directorate round to presenting his "red" plays, having prospered so much by putting on his "green" ones? Red and Green were inseparable, even in his earliest work, but the shade of red deepened and he seemed to leave his first admirers far behind him as he went exploring some world of artistic politics or of political art. If he had stayed in Dublin, steadily turning out a play every year or two for the Abbey, would he have been the same dramatist? It seems unlikely, but the divorce between him and Dublin was a tragedy. The Abbey retained custody of the first three children and it is noticeable that the companies of today seem to do better whenever there is a revival of "The Plough and the Stars" or "Juno and the Paycock" and can make more of "The Shadow of a Gunman" than used to be got out of it. O'Casey first fulfilled himself by working for the Abbey and the players there made his work peculiarly their own, just as they did Synge's—but the Abbey had to carry on its work after O'Casey left Ireland, just as they had to continue when Synge died.

Something in its earliest roots has given the Abbey strength to survive its troubles. It does sometimes seem that a theatre can develop a life of its own and a resistance to the usual theatrical tendency to change and decay. The Moscow Art Theatre is one astonishing example, for it was founded in 1898 and not, as so many people seem to think, some time after 1917 and Bolshoi was a great name in Russian ballet before Bolsheviks were ever heard of. The Old Vic in London has the same sort of strength. It not only keeps going year after year in the face of sometimes bitter and unkind criticism, it even proliferates so that we have two ballet companies and an opera all springing from roots which originally were no stronger than those of the Irish National Theatre Society. And if anybody is fond of apparent historical parallels he might ponder the fact that one of the birthplaces of the Abbey was the Coffee Palace in Townsend Street, where the Fays used to put on their rudimentary farces and comedies to satisfy the demands of the lively temperance movement of the late 19th century. And the original name of the Old Vic was the Royal Victoria Coffee Music Hall, for it too was originally a weapon against intemperance in a poor district of London.

This persistence of particular theatres is easier to understand in the European countries where a national theatre as a state foundation is taken for granted. That something comparable should have happened in Dublin in not much more than fifty years is more difficult to grasp. The Abbey Theatre is less beholden to the government than any other national theatre in the world: though the British are made fun of for failing to build their National Theatre, they subsidise the Royal Opera House alone by £250,000 a year and the Old Vic, even as a poor relation gets £25,000. The recent subsidy of the Abbey has been £8,000, and even allowing for contemporary dissatisfaction with the theatre no country in the world gets better value for so little money.

And now Dublin, having lost its original Abbey Theatre by fire in 1951 waits to see what will come of the plans for providing a new and larger theatre on roughly the same site.

One explanation given for the fire was that if the theatre had been able to afford £5 a week for a night watchman it could never have happened. How then, on the small amount of insurance money available could a theatre be built which will be larger, much larger, than the original Abbey? Government help has been promised and Mr. Michael Scott, the Irish architect, has cooperated with M. Pierre Sonrel a Frenchman who specialises in the design of theatres; (he remodelled the Old Vic when it was being repaired after the war). Several sets of plans have been drawn and one of them entirely abandoned. Difficulties about buying, at a reasonable price, the whole of the site required have caused a long delay, but unless there is a complete reversal of plans the new Abbey Theatre will be a striking building over a hundred feet high. That is equivalent to a 10 storey office block and it would make a remarkable new architectural composition standing only a couple of hundred yards away from the projected new Liberty Hall, which is to be a 16 storey tower.

There would be two theatres in the new Abbey—the main auditorium seating 800 and the smaller experimental theatre to replace the Peacock Theatre (the Abbey's miniature auditorium which was destroyed also). Since there are site restrictions even when the Abbey has brought into use some property surrounding the theatre, Scott has had the notion of putting the two theatres one on top of the other. This has never been done in Ireland before and seemed difficult to fit in with existing safety regulations. But the advice of the Paris Fire Brigade was sought, for they are familiar with such buildings, and a plan was arrived at which would allow the Scott-Sonrel theatre to be built and still satisfy the regulations.

It would be, of course, the most modern theatre in Europe and might set the pattern for theatre building elsewhere for many decades. It would have under its roof every single form of equipment required for staging a repertory of plays—the wardrobe, the property department, the scene-painting dock and every other element of a well-conducted theatre all in the right place and not fitted in afterwards by accident.

This is a long way from what Frank Fay once hoped for: "a theatre about as big as the stage of the Queen's" and it naturally has caused some misgivings about whether it is not too ambitious. What is wrong with a remodelling of the Queen's, some people ask, or even with remodelling the Abbey itself which was not entirely destroyed and could be fitted out again? It has been argued that the very cramped conditions of the Abbey stage and auditorium helped to create not only the special style of acting, but also the specially intimate relationship between the players and the audience. There are those, too, who see the move to the Queen's as the perfect compromise between a too confined theatre and one which would be big enough to swallow the present company.

I find it much less exciting to speculate about the shape of the new theatre than about what is to be staged in it. I have never been attached much to the notion that a theatre is a building in which a company of actors put on plays. A theatre is a company of actors plus what their dramatists give them to work with on the stage and when I think about the future of the Abbey Theatre it is plays and players rather than architects and plans that I put first.

The Irish theatre can feed for years on the work of writers like George Shiels, Lennox Robinson, Paul Vincent Carroll or Joseph Tomelty—for years, but not forever. An O'Casey is required once in every twenty years or so. He has not turned up lately. Nor in the more "classical" Abbey tradition is there the slightest sign of a successor to Yeats or Synge or Lady Gregory, and if one did turn up it is quite possible that his plays would not be particularly welcome.

If the Irish theatre has not been at its best for the last few years what might be expected to pull it up again? This is difficult to forecast except that I could make a good guess that it would be something not strictly theatrical. It is the pattern of drama in English-speaking countries to produce their best new plays and writers in times of national emotional excitement and stress. The Elizabethan-Jacobean time, the Restoration, the entry into the 20th century (though not, that century's great wars) show it in the English theatre. Until the Americans had the thrill of seeing their economy collapse in the 'thirties they produced hardly anything for the theatre which was not a carbon copy of something European (except Eugene O'Neill—and he stopped writing anything that mattered much at just about the same time as the newer American dramatists began to show themselves).

Ireland was excited between the 1890's and the 1920's by the abandonment of the Home Rule idea, the substitution of republicanism, the fighting against the British, the civil war between Irishmen. While these excitements lasted there was a dazzling outbreak of drama. But O'Casey was the last to produce original work successfully—and by original I mean not consciously imitated. If a new Abbey Theatre is built who are to be the original dramatists who will ensure that its future is as eventful as its past?

It is not by accident that I end this book with a question. I began it with one and I think I have given at least part of the answer to the query "why did Ireland throw up the dramatists, actors and organisers who could make a success of the Abbey Theatre?" I cannot answer, (and do not know who can) the infinitely more difficult question "What is the future of the Abbey Theatre and who will lead it into the future?"

BIBLIOGRAPHY

Dramatis Personae, by W. B. Yeats (1896-1902).

Hail and Farewell, by George Moore (1911).

The Death of Synge, by W. B. Yeats (1909).

Our Irish Theatre, by Lady Gregory (1914).

The Contemporary Drama of Ireland, by Ernest A. Boyd (1918).

The Story of Ireland's National Theatre, by Dawson Byrne (1929).

The Irish Drama, by Andrew E. Malone (1929).

The Fays of the Abbey Theatre, by W. G. Fay and Catherine Carswell (1935).

The Irish Dramatic Movement, by Una Ellis-Fermor (1939, second edition 1954).

W. B. Yeats, by Joseph Hone (1942).

J. B. Yeats, Letters to his son (1944).

Lady Gregory's Journals, edited by Lennox Robinson (1946).

Innisfallen Fare The Well, by Sean O'Casey (1949).

Ireland's Abbey Theatre, by Lennox Robinson (1951).

Miss Horniman and the Gaiety Theatre, Manchester, by Rex Pogson (1952).

The Letters of W. B. Yeats, edited by Allan Wade (1954).

The Splendid Years, by Maire nic Shiubhlaigh (1955).

Occasional publications: Bealtaine: Samhain: The Arrow.

BIOGRAPHIES

WILLIAM BUTLER YEATS, 1865-1939.

The colossus of the Irish Theatre movement. If his plays are neglected now they provided just over fifty years ago the first impetus leading towards a truly national Irish theatre, in spite of being written in English.

There is a trace of Yorkshire in his ancestry, but his own branch had deep roots in Sligo. His great-grandfather and father were both parsons, his father a painter, an author and a philosopher: so the ingredients of Yeat's talents for declamation, reasoning and self-expression can be traced in the family tree. J. B. Yeats, the father, married Susan Pollexfen and their first son was born in Sandymount in June 1865 and christened in Donnybrook church. When his father moved to London W. B. Y. went to school in Hammersmith, later to the High School in Harcourt Street, Dublin, but never to a university. He started to write before he had left school and began collecting the folk-lore and myths which were to flavour so many of his plays. His earliest plays "The Land of Heart's Desire" (1894), "The Countess Cathleen" (1899) and "The Shadowy Waters" (1897, revised 1906) were experiments, not particularly successful: Later, in "The Hour Glass" and "The King's Threshold" he showed the fruitful effect of closely studying the technique of the stage. But it was not so much his plays (in spite of "Kathleen ni Houlihan" and "The Pot of Broth") as his presence which so fortified the Abbey for its first few years. By 1916 his mind had settled on other problems. He had been a member of the Irish Republican Brotherhood, but was inactive politically. The Easter Rising wrenched his thoughts out of their more

154

peaceful vein into an interpretation of life as affected by violence. It is curious that he published no play on the theme. Towards the end of his life, as a senator and an academician he became one of his country's learned elders: in the rest of the world he was regarded as possibly the greatest poet of a century.

AUGUSTA, LADY GREGORY, 1852-1932.

Of the Persse family, widow of Sir William Gregory a former Governor of Ceylon. Her home at Coole Park, Gort, Co. Galway was one of the powerhouses of the early Abbey for she invited authors there to rest and write in peace. She devoted herself almost continuously from 1904 to the time of her death to the interests of the Abbey (finding energy enough on the side to campaign tenaciously for the return to Dublin of the Lane Pictures). In the early years she kept up a good supply of plays like "The Rising of the Moon", "Spreading the News," "The Workhouse Ward" and "Hyacinth Halvey" which are, however, seldom seen today. She also in the "Kiltartan Molière" provided the Abbey with new translations which were successfully absorbed into the Irish technique. Nobody in the whole history of the Abbey can be compared with Lady Gregory for devotion to duty. Was she in love with Yeats? It seems immaterial, as does the same question sometimes asked about Miss Horniman. Lady Gregory was in love with the Abbey Theatre. I met her twice only, both times at the theatre when I was playing a small part in "The Hour Glass". She was so like Queen Victoria (to my eyes) that I almost called her "Your Majesty". And the fantasy was not too far-fetched for she had a queenly way and she ruled the Abbey for years.

JOHN MILLINGTON SYNGE, 1871-1909.

Born near Dublin; went to Trinity College, studied at the Royal Irish Academy of Music where he reached professional standard. He had sufficient income to support himself as a young man in Paris where he could have lived in great comfort but preferred to be among the artists, where Yeats found him and realised that an important Irish writer was being wasted—could he have known how important? Synge came back to Ireland and continued his boyhood pursuit of walking around listening to what was being said by the country people. His studies in Wicklow and in Aran were the foundation of "In the Shadow of the Glen" and "The Playboy of the Western World". If he invented a language and accent for his Irish peasant plays it was, at least, nearer to nature than art had ever ventured before. He was a man always at odds with orthodoxy. Although it is difficult to understand today the passionate opposition aroused by the "Playboy" and even by "In the Shadow of the Glen" it is perfectly clear that had he lived he would never have knuckled under. Indeed, like O'Casey, all the signs were that he would not have continued long to live where his work was so little appreciated. His death in his mid-thirties, with only half his work done was the greatest single blow borne by the Abbey Theatre in its early years.

ANNIE ELIZABETH FREDERICKA HORNIMAN, 1860-1937.

There is no woman to whom the British and Irish repertory theatres owe more than to Miss Horniman. I have been able to show her as a disruptive influence on the early years of the Abbey, but it should never be forgotten that she was the one person without whom the theatre might not have been built. She did much to make Manchester a centre of serious theatre and it is even suggested that she inspired Miss Bayliss to make the Royal Victoria Coffee Music Hall (better known as the Old Vic) into a real theatre. Miss Horniman shared in the fortunes of the famous tea firm, studied for five years as an art student at the Slade School, was five years private secretary to W. B. Yeats, acted as backer in 1894 for the first production of Shaw's "Arms and the Man". When asked to write a "Who's Who" entry all she said about Dublin was that she "opened the Abbey Theatre, 1904, where were produced a number of Irish plays". About the Gaiety, Manchester, she was warmer and pointed out that in the 14 years 1907-1921 her theatre presented two hundred plays of which one hundred were new—such a ratio of originality must surely have been linked with the originality of her mind.

WILLIAM GEORGE FAY, 1872-1947.

Born in Dublin, educated in Marlborough Street School and Belvedere College. As a young man went out as "advance agent" for Lloyd's Mexican Circus, travelling about Ireland posting bills and arranging to hire fields. After that played small parts with obscure companies touring England and Ireland. At the same time studied electricity and was a trained electrician by the time he settled down in Dublin to work with his brother in developing their dramatic society. At the Abbey he was the only original member of the company to have any direct experience of the professional stage. When he left the Abbey he organised a company including his brother Frank, his wife Brigit O'Dempsey, Dudley Digges and Maire Quinn to play Abbey plays under the management of Charles Frohman in New York and Chicago. After 1909, with brief interludes in Birmingham, Nottingham and Glasgow, he settled in London and worked regularly as an actor or producer. He began making films in 1916 and his last notable part, shortly before he died, was that of Father Tom in "Odd Man Out".

FRANCIS JOHN FAY, 1870-1931.

Born in Dublin, the family originally under the name O'Fahy, came from Galway. Educated at Marlborough Street Model School, Dublin. Worked as a clerk-stenographer with a firm of accountants, Craig, Gardner. With his brother organised various dramatic societies, culminating in the Irish National Theatre Society.

After leaving Dublin he spent some years touring England with Shakespearean companies and played for some seasons at the Birmingham Repertory Theatre. He returned to Dublin in 1921 and remained there until his death teaching acting and

---

elocution and producing plays in schools and colleges. He appeared from time to time at the Abbey Theatre in the 'twenties but never returned to the permanent company. For several years he did Saturday night poetry recitals on Radio Eireann and produced some of the first plays put out from the station. He also played a leading part in one of the first full-length films made in Ireland—"Wicklow Gold".

SARAH ALLGOOD, 1883-1950.

Probably Frank Fay's most successful pupil, with the exception of Dudley Digges, though he worked on her for only a short time. However she used to put it on record that she was "prepared for the stage by Frank J. Fay". She was early on the scene, appearing first at the Molesworth Hall in 1901 in "Twenty Five". She quickly ascended in the scale until she was playing leading parts. In 1913 she left the Abbey and after a time in the permanent company of the Liverpool Repertory Theatre and a visit to Miss Horniman's Manchester Gaiety she freelanced on the English stage successfully. For an actress of such quality, who created some of the finest parts of the Irish theatre it was a depressing fact that her most successful part when on tour in Australia was as Peg in "Peg o' My Heart". She reached her greatest tragic power as Juno in "Juno and the Paycock" and for a whole generation of Abbey-goers destroyed anybody else's chance of playing it convincingly—as Edith Evans, on the London stage, made it impossible (or at least indiscreet) for any other actress to tackle Lady Bracknell. To many theatregoers in England and America Sarah Allgood's is one of the names which sums up the chief virtues of the "Abbey school" of acting.

MAIRE O'NEILL, 1885-1952.

Sister of Sarah Allgood and wife of Arthur Sinclair. Her first husband, George Mair, was a "Manchester Guardian" man who seems to have been responsible for suggesting that C. P. Scott should act as arbitrator between the Abbey directors and Miss Horniman when they were having their final quarrel.

Like her sister Maire O'Neill, worked at first with the Abbey company and had a hand in some of the most historic of the early productions. She left Dublin in 1913, and made straight for New York before settling down for a few years in the English theatre. The combination of her acting and Lennox Robinson's writing made the first production of "The Whiteheaded Boy" at the Abbey one of the most heartening occasions for many years. She divided her time equally between Dublin, London and New York and had no competitor but her sister when it came to playing O'Casey parts, to which she constantly returned. Her two last appearances took her right back to the beginnings of the Abbey—she played Maurya in "Riders to the Sea" and Mary Byrne in "The Tinker's Wedding" in London in 1950.

PADRAIC COLUM.

Born 1881 in Co. Longford. Editor of the Irish Review and an original member of the Irish National Theatre Society. His play "Broken Soil" produced 1903. He emigrated to the U.S. in 1914 and has spent his life there, rarely returning to Ireland. He has published many volumes of verse and edited a monumental "Anthology of Irish Poetry".

DOUGLAS HYDE, 1860-1949.

Founder of the Gaelic League and one of the first moving spirits in providing plays in Irish for the national theatre. His Casadh an tSúgáin, produced by the Irish Literary Theatre, first brought W. G. Fay into direct contact with some of those who were later to become his colleagues in the Abbey Theatre. Douglas Hyde became first President of Ireland.

GEORGE MOORE, 1852-1933.

Lived in Paris as a young man and tried to become a painter, but found that his true talent was writing and turned to it successfully. The theatre fascinated him but he was more attracted to the professional stage of London than to the Art Theatre conceptions of Yeats and the Fays: therefore after his brief association with the Irish Literary Theatre he remained on the sidelines and Yeats was ready to go to any length to keep him out of the Abbey. Nevertheless he devoted a number of amusing inaccurate pages of "Ave" to his impressions of what went on in the earliest years of the Irish national theatre.

ACKNOWLEDGMENTS

I have had much generous help in finding the raw material for this book. For permission to quote from documents (and in some cases for help in finding them) I am indebted to Mrs. W. B. Yeats, the late Mr. Edward M. Stephens, Dr. Lennox Robinson and the late Mr. Allan Wade. In the difficult business of tracking down matters affecting Miss Horniman I was helped by Mr. Rex Pogson, Miss Philippa Steele, Miss Fanny Baker, Mr. Cartaret Rust and the Public Trustee. Some of the material about W. G. Fay and Brigit O'Dempsey is used by permission of Mr. D. W. Fay: Mr. David Greene made some important suggestions about J. M. Synge and Mr. P. J. Stephenson, chief Librarian of the City of Dublin Public Libraries pointed out to me important material on the origins of the Abbey Theatre premises. I am especially indebted for help and encouragement to Mr. Patrick Lynch, Professor Desmond Williams and Mr. Valentin Iremonger: for secretarial help to Miss J. E. McCulloch, for reading the proofs to my wife and for preparing the index to Lord Wicklow. Mr. Ernest Blythe helped me with the list of plays.

PLAY LIST

1899

PRODUCED BY THE IRISH LITERARY THEATRE
(at the Antient Concert Rooms, Brunswick Street, now Pearse Street.)

May: THE COUNTESS CATHLEEN ... *W. B. Yeats*

THE HEATHER FIELD   ... *Edward Martyn*

1900
(at the Gaiety Theatre)

February: THE BENDING OF THE BOUGH *George Moore*

THE LAST FEAST OF THE FIANNA *Alice Milligan*

MAEVE ...   . *Edward Martyn*

1901
(at the Gaiety Theatre)

October: DIARMUID AND GRÁINNE   ... *W. B. Yeats and George Moore*

CASADH AN TSÚGÁIN   ... *Douglas Hyde*

1902

PRODUCED BY W. G. FAY'S IRISH NATIONAL DRAMATIC CO. AT ST. THERESA'S HALL, CLARENDON STREET

April: DEIRDRE ...   . *"A.E."*
                                          (*G. W. Russell*)

           KATHLEEN NI HOULIHAN   ... *W. B. Yeats*

PRODUCED BY THE I.N.D.C.
AT THE ANTIENT CONCERT ROOMS

October: THE SLEEP OF THE KING ... *James Cousins*
           THE LAYING OF THE FOUND-
               ATIONS   ...   ... *Fred Ryan*
           A POT OF BROTH ...   ... *W. B. Yeats*
           THE RACING LUG   ... *James Cousins*
           EILÍS AGUS AN BHEAN DÉIRCE *Peadar Mac Fhionn-
                                        laoich*
                                       (*P. T. McGinley*)

(these plays were repeated by the IRISH NATIONAL THEATRE SOCIETY at 34 Lower Camden Street on December 4, 5 & 6, 1902)

1903

PRODUCED BY THE I.N.T.S. AT THE MOLESWORTH HALL

March: THE HOUR GLASS ...   ... *W. B. Yeats*
           TWENTY FIVE   ...   ... *Lady Gregory*
October: THE KING'S THRESHOLD   ... *W. B. Yeats*
           IN THE SHADOW OF THE GLEN *J. M. Synge*
December: BROKEN SOIL   ...   ... *Padraic Colum*

1904

PRODUCED BY THE I.N.T.S. AT THE MOLESWORTH HALL

January:	THE SHADOWY WATERS	... *W. B. Yeats*
	THE TOWNLAND OF TAMNEY	... *Seumas MacManus*
February:	RIDERS TO THE SEA	... *J. M. Synge*

PRODUCED BY THE I.N.T.S. AT THE ABBEY THEATRE

December:	ON BAILE'S STRAND	... *W. B. Yeats*
	SPREADING THE NEWS	... *Lady Gregory*

1905

February:	THE WELL OF THE SAINTS	... *J. M. Synge*
March:	KINCORA ...	... *Lady Gregory*
April:	THE BUILDING FUND	... *William Boyle*
June:	THE LAND ...	... *Padraic Colum*
December:	THE WHITE COCKADE	... *Lady Gregory*

1906

January:	THE ELOQUENT DEMPSEY	... *William Boyle*
February:	HYACINTH HALVEY	... *Lady Gregory*
April:	THE DOCTOR IN SPITE OF HIMSELF	*Molière (Translated by Lady Gregory)*
October:	THE GAOL GATE	... *Lady Gregory*
	THE MINERAL WORKERS	... *William Boyle*
November:	DEIRDRE	... *W. B. Yeats*
December:	THE CANAVANS ...	... *Lady Gregory*
	THE SHADOWY WATERS (Revised)	... *W. B. Yeats*

1907

January:	THE PLAYBOY OF THE WESTERN WORLD	... J. M. Synge
February:	THE JACKDAW	... Lady Gregory
March:	THE RISING OF THE MOON	... Lady Gregory
	THE INTERIOR	... Maurice Maeterlinck
April:	THE EYES OF THE BLIND	... Winifred Letts
	THE POORHOUSE	... Lady Gregory and Douglas Hyde
	FAND	... Wilfred Scawen Blunt
October:	THE COUNTRY DRESSMAKER	George Fitzmaurice
	DERVORGILLA	... Lady Gregory
November:	THE UNICORN FROM THE STARS	W. B. Yeats and Lady Gregory

1908

February:	THE MAN WHO MISSED THE TIDE	... W. F. Casey
	THE PIPER	... Norreys Connell (Conal O'Riordan)
March:	THE PIE-DISH	... George Fitzmaurice
	THE GOLDEN HELMET	... W. B. Yeats
	TEJA	... Sudermann
April:	THE ROGUERIES OF SCAPIN	... Molière (Translated by Lady Gregory)
	THE WORKHOUSE WARD	... Lady Gregory
May:	THE SCHEMING LIEUTENANT	... Richard Brinsley Sheridan
October:	THE SUBURBAN GROOVE	... W. F. Casey
	THE CLANCY NAME	... Lennox Robinson
	WHEN THE DAWN IS COME	... Thomas MacDonagh

1909

January:	THE MISER ...	... *Molière (Translated by Lady Gregory)*
March:	STEPHEN GRAY ...	... *D. L. Kelleher*
April:	THE CROSS ROADS	... *Lennox Robinson*
	TIME	... *Norreys Connell (Conal O'Riordan)*
	THE GLITTERING GATE	... *Lord Dunsany*
May:	AN IMAGINARY CONVERSATION	*Norreys Connell (Conal O'Riordan)*
August:	THE SHEWING-UP OF BLANCO POSNET ...	... *Bernard Shaw*
September:	THE WHITE FEATHER	... *R. J. Ray*
October:	THE CHALLENGE ...	... *Winifred Letts*
November:	THE IMAGE ...	... *Lady Gregory*

1910

January:	DEIRDRE OF THE SORROWS ...	*J. M. Synge*
February:	THE GREEN HELMET	... *W. B. Yeats*
	MIRANDOLINA ...	... *Goldoni (Translated by Lady Gregory)*
March:	THE TRAVELLING MAN	... *Lady Gregory*
May:	THOMAS MUSKERRY	... *Padraic Colum*
	HARVEST ...	... *Lennox Robinson*
September:	THE CASTING-OUT OF MARTIN WHELAN ...	... *R. J. Ray*
October:	BIRTHRIGHT ...	... *T. C. Murray*
November:	THE FULL MOON ...	... *Lady Gregory*
	THE SHUILER'S CHILD	... *Seumas O'Kelly*
December:	COATS	... *Lady Gregory*

1911

January:	NATIVITY PLAY ...	... *Douglas Hyde*
	THE DELIVERER ...	... *Lady Gregory*
	KING ARGIMENES AND THE UN-	
	KNOWN WARRIOR	... *Lord Dunsany*
	THE LAND OF HEART'S DESIRE	*W. B. Yeats*
	MIXED MARRIAGE	... *St. John G. Ervine*
November:	THE INTERLUDE OF YOUTH ...	*Anon.*
	THE SECOND SHEPHERD'S PLAY	*Anon.*
	THE MARRIAGE ...	... *Douglas Hyde*
December:	RED TURF ...	... *Rutherford Mayne*

1912

January:	THE ANNUNCIATION	... *Anon.*
	THE FLIGHT INTO EGYPT	... *Anon.*
	McDONOUGH'S WIFE	... *Lady Gregory*
	AN TINCÉAR AGUS AN TSÍDHEÓG	*Douglas Hyde*
	THE WORLDE AND THE CHYLDE	*Anon.*
March:	FAMILY FAILING ...	... *William Boyle*
April:	PATRIOTS ...	... *Lennox Robinson*
	JUDGMENT ...	... *Joseph Campbell*
June:	MAURICE HARTE ...	... *T. C. Murray*
July:	THE BOGIE MAN ...	... *Lady Gregory*
September:	THE COUNTESS CATHLEEN ...	*W. B. Yeats*
October:	THE MAGNANIMOUS LOVER ...	*St. John G. Ervine*
November:	DAMER'S GOLD ...	... *Lady Gregory*
December:	A LITTLE CHRISTMAS MIRACLE	*E. Hamilton Moore*

1913

January:	THE CUCKOO'S NEST ...	*John Guinan*
	THE DEAN OF ST. PATRICK'S	*G. Sidney Paternoster*
February:	HANNELE	*Gerhardt Hauptmann*
March:	THERE ARE CRIMES AND CRIMES	*August Strindberg*
April:	THE HOMECOMING ...	*Gertrude Robins*
	THE STRONGER	*August Strindberg*
	THE MAGIC GLASSES ...	*George Fitzmaurice*
	BROKEN FAITH	*S. R. Day and G. D. Cummins*
May:	THE POST OFFICE ...	*Rabindranath Tagore*
June:	THE GOMBEEN MAN ...	*R. J. Ray*
September:	SOVEREIGN LOVE	*T. C. Murray*
October:	THE MINE LAND	*Joseph Connolly*
	MY LORD	*Mrs. Bart Kennedy*
November:	THE CRITICS	*St. John G. Ervine*
December:	DUTY	*Seumas O'Brien*
	THE BRIBE	*Seumas O'Kelly*

1914

January:	DAVID MAHONY ...	*Victor O'D. Power*
March:	THE ORANGEMEN	*St. John G. Ervine*
	THE LORD MAYOR	*Edward McNulty*
April:	KINSHIP	*J. Bernard MacCarthy*
	THE COBBLER ...	*A. Patrick Wilson*
August:	A MINUTE'S WAIT ...	*Martin J. MacHugh*
September:	THE SUPPLANTER ...	*J. Bernard MacCarthy*
	THE DARK HOUR ...	*R. A. Christie*
	THE CROSSING ...	*Con O'Leary*
	THE PRODIGAL ...	*Walter Riddall*
October:	THE COBWEB ...	*F. Jay*
	THE JUG OF SORROW	*W. P. Ryan*
November:	THE SLOUGH ...	*A. Patrick Wilson*
December:	THE CRITIC ...	*R. B. Sheridan*

1915

January:	By Word of Mouth	... *F. C. Moore and W. P. Flanagan*
February:	The Dreamers ...	... *Lennox Robinson*
April:	The Bargain ...	... *William Crone*
	The Philosopher	... *Martin J. MacHugh*
	Shanwalla ...	... *Lady Gregory*
November:	John Ferguson ...	... *St. John G. Ervine*

1916

January:	Fraternity ...	... *Bernard Duffy*
February:	The Coiner ...	... *Bernard Duffy*
March:	The Plough Lifters	... *John Guinan*
September:	John Bull's Other Island	... *Bernard Shaw*
October:	Widower's Houses	... *Bernard Shaw*
	Arms and the Man	... *Bernard Shaw*
	Nic	... *William Boyle*
November:	Partition ...	... *D. C. Maher*
December:	The Counter Charm	... *Bernard Duffy*
	The Whiteheaded Boy	... *Lennox Robinson*

In his "Abbey Plays" Brinsley MacNamara has this note:

PLAY ANNOUNCED

BUT NEVER PRODUCED

THE SPANCEL OF DEATH

T. H. Nally

The date upon which this play was to have been produced was the Easter Monday of the Insurrection in Dublin in 1916. No attempt was afterwards made to stage the play.

1917

January:	TOMMY-TOM-TOM ...	... *Martin J. MacHugh*
	THE CRUSADERS ...	... *J.Bernard MacCarthy*
February:	FOX AND GEESE ...	... *S. R. Day and G. D. Cummins*
	MAN AND SUPERMAN	... *Bernard Shaw*
March:	THE INCA OF PERUSALEM	... *Bernard Shaw*
April:	THE STRONG HAND	... *R. J. Ray*
May:	THE DOCTOR'S DILEMMA	... *Bernard Shaw*
September:	THE PARNELLITE ...	... *Seumas O'Kelly*
October:	THE BACACH ...	... *John Barnewall*
November:	THE SPOILING OF WILSON	... *R. J. Purcell*
	FRIENDS	... *Herbert Farjeon*
December:	BLIGHT	... *'Alpha and Omega'*

1918

January:	SPRING	... *T. C. Murray*
	WHEN LOVE CAME OVER THE HILLS	*W. R. Fearon and* ... *Roy Nesbitt*
	HANRAHAN'S OATH	... *Lady Gregory*
February:	THE LOST LEADER	... *Lennox Robinson*
March:	ALIENS	... *Rose McKenna*
May:	A LITTLE BIT OF YOUTH	... *C. Callister*
September:	SABLE AND GOLD ...	... *Maurice Dalton*
November:	THE GRABBER ...	... *E. F. Barrett*
December:	ATONEMENT ...	... *Dorothy Macardle*

1919

March:	THE REBELLION IN BALLY-CULLEN	... Brinsley MacNamara
April:	THE DRAGON ...	... Lady Gregory
August:	BRADY	... Sadie Casey
	THE FIDDLER'S HOUSE	... Padraic Colum
	A SERIOUS THING	... Gideon Ousley
September:	THE SAINT ...	... Desmond Fitzgerald
	A NIGHT AT AN INN	... Lord Dunsany
	THE LABOUR LEADER	... Daniel Corkery
October:	MEADOWSWEET ...	... Seumas O'Kelly
	QUEER ONES ...	... Con O'Leary
November:	ANDROCLES AND THE LION	... Bernard Shaw
	THE ENCHANTED TROUSERS	... Gideon Ousley
December:	THE PLAYER QUEEN	... W. B. Yeats

1920

January:	THE GOLDEN APPLE	... Lady Gregory
February:	THE DEVIL'S DISCIPLE	... Bernard Shaw
	THE DAEMON IN THE HOUSE	... F. Barrington
April:	THE GOOD-NATURED MAN	... Oliver Goldsmith
May:	THE YELLOW BITTERN	... Daniel Corkery
	THE TENTS OF THE ARABS	... Lord Dunsany
August:	THE WOOING OF JULIA ELIZABETH ...	... James Stephens
September:	THE DRIFTERS ...	... F. H. O'Donnell
	A ROYAL ALLIANCE	... Fergus O'Nolan
October:	THE SERF ...	... Stephen Morgan
	THE ISLAND OF SAINTS	... St. John G. Ervine
November:	THE LAND FOR THE PEOPLE	... Brinsley MacNamara
December:	CANDLE AND CRIB	... K. F. Purdon

1921

January:	BEDMATES ...	... *George Shiels*
February:	THE REVOLUTIONIST	... *Terence MacSwiney*
March:	ARISTOTLE'S BELLOWS	... *Lady Gregory*
October:	THE PERFECT DAY	... *Emile Mazaud*
	A MERRY DEATH	... *Nicholas Evreinov*
November:	THE COURTING OF MARY DOYLE ...	... *Edward McNulty*
	THE PIPER OF TAVRAN	... *Bernard Duffy*
December:	INSURANCE MONEY	... *George Shiels*

1922

January:	AFTERMATH ...	... *T. C. Murray*
	THE ROUND TABLE	... *Lennox Robinson*
March:	THE MAN OF DESTINY	... *Bernard Shaw*
April:	THE YOUNG MAN FROM RATHMINES ...	... *M. M. Brennan*
	ANN KAVANAGH ...	... *Dorothy Macardle*
August:	THE MORAL LAW	... *R. J. Ray*
September:	THE LEPRECAUN IN THE TENEMENT	... *M. M. Brennan*
October:	PAUL TWYNING ...	... *George Shiels*
	THE GRASSHOPPER	... *Padraic Colum*
November:	CRABBED YOUTH AND AGE ...	*Lennox Robinson*

1923

January:	THE LONG ROAD TO GARRAN-BRAHER	J. Bernard MacCarthy
March:	'TWIXT THE GILTINANS AND THE CARMODYS	George Fitzmaurice
	A DOLL'S HOUSE ...	Henrik Ibsen
April:	THE SHADOW OF A GUNMAN ...	Seán O'Casey
	SHE STOOPS TO CONQUER ...	Oliver Goldsmith
September:	APARTMENTS ...	Fand O'Grady
October:	CATHLEEN LISTENS-IN ...	Seán O'Casey
November:	THE GLORIOUS UNCERTAINTY	Brinsley MacNamara
December:	FIRST AID ...	George Shiels
	THE OLD WOMAN REMEMBERS	Lady Gregory

1924

February:	NEVER THE TIME AND THE PLACE ...	Lennox Robinson
	THE TWO SHEPHERDS ...	G. M. Sierra
March:	JUNO AND THE 'PAYCOCK' ...	Seán O'Casey
April:	THE STORY BROUGHT BY BRIGIT	Lady Gregory
May:	THE RETRIEVERS ...	George Sheils
September:	AUTUMN FIRE ...	T. C. Murray
	NANNIE'S NIGHT OUT ...	Seán O'Casey
November:	THE KINGDOM OF GOD ...	G. M. Sierra
December:	THE PASSING ...	Kenneth Sarr
	OLD MAG ...	Kenneth Sarr

1925

February:	THE OLD MAN ...	Dorothy Macardle
March:	ANTI-CHRIST ...	F. H. O'Donnell
	PORTRAIT ...	Lennox Robinson
April:	FANNY'S FIRST PLAY ...	Bernard Shaw
	THE PROPOSAL ...	Anton Tchekov
September:	PROFESSOR TIM ...	George Shiels
October:	THE WHITE BLACKBIRD	Lennox Robinson

1926

January:	THE WOULD-BE GENTLEMAN	*Molière (Translated by Lady Gregory)*
February:	THE PLOUGH AND THE STARS	*Seán O'Casey*
	DOCTOR KNOCK ...	... *Jules Romains*
April:	LOOK AT THE HEFFERNANS ...	... *Brinsley MacNamara*
August:	MR. MURPHY'S ISLAND	... *Elizabeth Harte*
September:	THE BIG HOUSE ...	... *Lennox Robinson*
November:	THE IMPORTANCE OF BEING EARNEST ...	... *Oscar Wilde*
December:	OEDIPUS THE KING	... *Sophocles-Yeats*

1927

January:	THE EMPEROR JONES	... *Eugene O'Neill*
	TRIFLES	... *Susan Glaspell*
March:	SANCHO'S MASTER	... *Lady Gregory*
April:	PARTED ...	... *M. C. Madden*
May:	DAVE	... *Lady Gregory*
	BLACK OLIVER ...	... *John Guinan*
July:	THE ROUND TABLE	... *Lennox Robinson*
August:	THE DRAPIER LETTERS	... *Arthur Power*
September:	OEDIPUS AT COLONNUS	... *Sophocles-Yeats*
October:	THE PIPE IN THE FIELDS	... *T. C. Murray*
	CAESAR AND CLEOPATRA	... *Bernard Shaw*
November:	CARTNEY AND KEVNEY	... *George Shiels*

1928

March:	THE MASTER ...	... *Brinsley MacNamara*
April:	JOHN GABRIEL BORKMAN	... *Henrik Ibsen*
	THE BLIND WOLF	... *T. C. Murray*
July:	BEFORE MIDNIGHT	... *Gerald Brosnan*
Agust:	FULL MEASURE ...	... *Cathleen M. O'Brennan*
October:	THE FAR-OFF HILLS	... *Lennox Robinson*
November:	THE WOMEN HAVE THEIR WAY	*Quintero Brothers*
	KING LEAR ...	... *William Shakespeare*

1929

March:	MOUNTAIN DEW ...	... *George Shiels*
August:	FIGHTING THE WAVES	... *W. B. Yeats*
September:	THE WOMAN ...	... *Margaret O'Leary*
October:	EVER THE TWAIN	... *Lennox Robinson*
	THE GODS OF THE MOUNTAIN	*Lord Dunsany*
December:	DARK ISLE ...	... *Gerald Brosnan*

1930

January:	PETER	... *Rutherford Mayne*
March:	THE REAPERS ...	... *Teresa Deevy*
April:	THE NEW GOSSOON	... *George Shiels*
September:	LET THE CREDIT GO	... *Bryan Cooper*
November:	THE WORDS UPON THE WINDOW PANE ...	... *W. B. Yeats*

1931

January:	THE CRITIC ...	... *Sheridan-Robinson*
February:	THE RUNE OF HEALING	... *John Guinan*
	PETER THE LIAR ...	... *A. Leprovost*
March:	MONEY	... *Hugh P. Quinn*
April:	THE MOON IN THE YELLOW	
	RIVER	... *Denis Johnston*
June:	THE ADMIRABLE BASHVILLE ...	*Bernard Shaw*
July:	SCRAP	... *J. A. O'Brennan*
August:	A DISCIPLE ...	... *Teresa Deevy*
September:	THE CAT AND THE MOON ...	*W. B. Yeats*
December:	THE DREAMING OF THE BONES	*W. B. Yeats*

1932

June:	MICHAELMAS EVE ...	... *T. C. Murray*
July:	ALL'S OVER THEN	... *Lennox Robinson*
August:	THINGS THAT ARE CAESAR'S	*Paul Vincent Carroll*
September:	TEMPORAL POWERS ...	... *Teresa Deevy*
October:	THE MATING OF SHAN M'GHIE	*G. H. Stafford*
	VIGIL	... *A. P. Fanning*
	THE WILD DUCK	... *Henrik Ibsen*
November:	THE BIG SWEEP ...	... *M. M. Brennan*
	SHERIDAN'S MILLS	... *Norman Webb*
	WRACK	... *Peadar O'Donnell*

1933

February:	DRAMA AT INISH ...	... *Lennox Robinson*
March:	MEN CROWD ME ROUND	... *Francis Stuart*
July:	MARGARET GILLAN	... *Brinsley MacNamara*
	THE DRINKING HORN	... *Arthur Duff*
August:	THE JEZEBEL ...	... *J. K. Montgomery*
September:	1920	... *F. X. O'Leary*
November:	GROGAN AND THE FERRET ...	*George Shiels*
December:	YOU NEVER CAN TELL	... *Bernard Shaw*

1934

February:	THE MARRIAGE PACKET	... *Arthur Power*
April:	DAYS WITHOUT END	... *Eugene O'Neill*
May:	CHURCH STREET ...	... *Lennox Robinson*
June:	BRIDGEHEAD	... *Rutherford Mayne*
July:	ON THE ROCKS ...	... *Bernard Shaw*
	THE RESURRECTION	... *W. B. Yeats*
	THE KING OF THE GREAT CLOCK TOWER ...	... *W. B. Yeats*
October:	PARNELL OF AVONDALE	... *W. R. Fearon*
	MACBETH	... *William Shakespeare*
November:	GALLANT CASSIAN	... *Arthur Schnitzler*
	THE SCHOOL FOR WIVES	... *Molière*
December:	SIX CHARACTERS IN SEARCH OF AN AUTHOR	... *Luigi Pirandello*
	AT MRS. BEAM'S	... *G. K. Munro*

1935

April:	THE KING OF SPAIN'S DAUGHTER ...	... *Teresa Deevy*
August:	THE SILVER TASSIE	... *Seán O'Casey*
September:	A DEUCE OF JACKS	... *F. R. Higgins*
	A VILLAGE WOOING	... *Bernard Shaw*
	CANDIDA	... *Bernard Shaw*
November:	NOAH ...	... *André Obey*
December:	A SAINT IN A HURRY	... *Penám-de Blácam*
	SUMMER'S DAY ...	... *Maura Molloy*

1936

January:	CORIOLANUS ...	... *William Shakespeare*
February:	THE GRAND HOUSE IN THE CITY	... *Brinsley MacNamara*
	BOYD'S SHOP ...	... *St. John G. Ervine*
March:	KATIE ROCHE ...	... *Teresa Deevy*
April:	THE PASSING DAY	... *George Shiels*
June:	HASSAN	... *James Elroy Flecker*
September:	THE SILVER JUBILEE	... *Cormac O'Daly*
October:	THE JAILBIRD ...	... *George Shiels*
November:	THE WILD GOOSE	... *Teresa Deevy*
	WIND FROM THE WEST	... *Maeve O'Callaghan*
December:	BLIND MAN'S BUFF	... *Johnston-Toller*

1937

January:	SHADOW AND SUBSTANCE ...	*Paul Vincent Carroll*
February:	THE END OF THE BEGINNING	*Seán O'Casey*
March:	QUIN'S SECRET ...	... *George Shiels*
April:	KILLYCREGGS IN TWILIGHT ...	*Lennox Robinson*
May:	WHO WILL REMEMBER . . .?	*Maura Molloy*
	IN THE TRAIN ...	... *Frank O'Connor and Hugh Hunt*
August:	THE PATRIOT ...	... *Maeve O'Callaghan*
September:	THE MAN IN THE CLOAK	... *Louis D'Alton*
October:	THE INVINCIBLES ...	... *Hugh Hunt and Frank O'Connor*
November:	CARTNEY AND KEVNEY	... *George Shiels*
	COGGERERS ...	... *Paul Vincent Carroll*
December:	SHE HAD TO DO SOMETHING ...	*Seán Ó'Faoláin*

M

1938

January:	NEAL MAQUADE ...	... *George Shiels*
February:	A SPOT IN THE SUN	... *T. C. Murray*
	MOSES' ROCK ...	... *Hugh Hunt and Frank O'Connor*
April:	THE DEAR QUEEN	... *Andrew Ganly*
August:	PURGATORY ...	... *W. B. Yeats*
September:	BIRD'S NEST ...	... *Lennox Robinson*
	THE GREAT ADVENTURE	... *Charles I. Foley*
October:	PILGRIMS	... *Mary Rynne*
December:	BAINTIGHEARNA AN GHORTA	*Séamus Wilmot*
	TIME'S POCKET ...	... *Frank O'Connor*

1939

February:	CAESAR'S IMAGE ...	... *E. F. Carey*
March:	TOMORROW NEVER COMES ...	... *Louis D'Alton*
April:	THE HERITAGE ...	... *J. K. Montgomery*
May:	DONNCHADH RUADH	... *Séamus Ó hAodha*
July:	ILLUMINATION ...	... *T. C. Murray*
August:	FOHNAM THE SCULPTOR	... *Daniel Corkery*
September:	KINDRED ...	... *Paul Vincent Carroll*
October:	GIVE HIM A HOUSE	... *George Shiels*
December:	THEY WENT BY THE BUS	... *Frank Carney*

1940

January:	THE SPANISH SOLDIER	... *Louis D'Alton*
March:	WILLIAM JOHN MAWHINNEY	*St. John G. Ervine*
April:	MOUNT PROSPECT ...	... *Elizabeth Connor*
May:	THE BIRTH OF A GIANT	... *Nora MacAdam*
July:	TO-DAY AND YESTERDAY	... *W. D. Hepenstall*
August:	THE RUGGED PATH	... *George Shiels*
November:	THREE TO GO ...	... *Olga Fielden*
	PEEPING TOM ...	... *Frank Carney*
December:	STRANGE GUEST ...	... *Francis Stuart*

1941

January:	TRIAL AT GREEN STREET COURT HOUSE ...	... *Roger McHugh*
February:	THE SUMMIT ...	... *George Shiels*
March:	THE MONEY DOESN'T MATTER	*Louis D'Alton*
May:	THE LADY IN THE TWILIGHT	*Mervyn Wall*
June:	FRIENDS AND RELATIONS	... *St. John G. Ervine*
August:	REMEMBERED FOR EVER	... *Bernard McGinn*
September:	THE FIRE BURNS LATE	... *P. J. Fitzgibbon*
	SWANS AND GEESE	... *Elizabeth Connor*
October:	LOVERS' MEETING	... *Louis D'Alton*
November:	THE THREE THIMBLES	... *Brinsley MacNamara*
December:	FORGET ME NOT	... *Lennox Robinson*
	BLACK FAST ...	... *Austin Clarke*

1942

February:	GLOINE AN IMPIRE	... *Traolach Ó Raith-bheartaigh*
	CÁCH	... *Earnán de Blaghd*
March:	THE CURSING FIELDS	... *Andrew Ganly*
April:	THE SINGER ...	... *Pádraic Pearse*
	THE FORT FIELD ...	... *George Shiels*
May:	LA LA NOO ...	... *Jack B. Yeats*
July:	THE WHIP HAND ...	... *B. G. MacCarthy*
September:	AN APPLE A DAY	... *Elizabeth Connor*
November:	AN STOIRM ...	... *Ostrovsky-Mac Dhubháin*

1943

January:	Faustus Kelly ...	... *Myles na gCopaleen*
	An Bhean Chródha	... *Piaras Béaslaoi*
February:	Ar an mBóthar Mór	... *Bernard-Ó Briain*
March:	The O'Cuddy ...	... *Anthony Wharton*
	Assembly At Druim Ceat ...	*Roibeárd Ó Farachain* (*Robert Farren*)
April:	An Coimisinéar ...	... *Tomás Ó Suilleabháin*
	Old Road ...	... *Michael J. Molloy*
	Lost Light ...	... *Roibeárd Ó Farachain* (*Robert Farren*)
May:	An Traona Sa Mhóinfhéar	*Séamus de Faoite-Ó hAnnracháin*
August:	Thy Dear Father	... *Gerard Healy*
October:	Ordóg an Bháis	... *Micheál Ó hAodha*
December:	Poor Man's Miracle	... *Marian Hemar*

1944

January:	Laistiar De'n Éadan	... *Eibhlín Ní Shuileabháin*
February:	The Wise Have Not Spoken	*Paul Vincent Carroll*
March:	The New Régime	... *George Shiels*
	Stiana	... *Peadar Ó hAnnracháin*
May:	The Coloured Balloon ...	*Margaret O'Leary*
	Sodar I nDiaidh Na nUasal	*Molière-de Blaghd*
August:	The End House ...	... *Joseph Tomelty*
October:	Railway House	... *Ralph Kennedy*
November:	Borumha Laighean	... *Seán Ó Conchobhair*

1945

January:	AN T-UBHALL ÓIR	... Gregory-Ó Briain
March:	GIOLLA AN TSOLUIS	... Máiread Ní Ghráda
	ROSSA	... Roger McHugh
May:	AN T-ÚDAR I NGLEIC	... Labhrás Mac Brádaigh
August:	MARKS AND MABEL	... Brinsley MacNamara
September:	TENANTS AT WILL	... George Shiels
	NUAIR A BHÍONN FEAR MARBH	Fauchois-Ó Briain
December:	MUIREANN AGUS AN PRIONNSA	Micheál Ó hAodha

1946

February:	MUNGO'S MANSION	... Walter Macken
March:	THE OLD BROOM	... George Shiels
April:	CAITLÍN NÍ UALLACHÁIN	... Yeats-Luibhéid
July:	THE RIGHTEOUS ARE BOLD	... Frank Carney
November:	THE VISITING HOUSE	... Michael J. Molloy
December:	FERNANDO AGUS AN DRAGAN	———

1947

February:	THEY GOT WHAT THEY WANTED ...	... Louis D'Alton
May:	THE DARK ROAD ...	... Elizabeth Connor
	OÍCHE MHAITH AGAT, A MHIC UÍ DHOMHNAILL	... Brennan-O Briain
August:	THE GREAT PACIFICATOR	... Sigerson Clifford
November:	DIARMUID AGUS GRÁINNE	... Micheál MacLiammóir

1948

January:	RÉALT DHIARMUDA ...	———
February:	THE CARETAKERS ...	... *George Shiels*
March:	MÁIRE RÓS ...	... *Barrie-Nic Chionnaith*
July:	THE DRUMS ARE OUT	... *John Coulter*
August:	ARÍS	... *Gheón-Ó Briain*
	THE LUCKY FINGER	... *Lennox Robinson*
October:	NA CLOIGÍNÍ ...	... *Erckmann-Chatrian, Nic Mhaicín*
	THE KING OF FRIDAY'S MEN	*M. J. Molloy*
December:	BRIAN AGUS AN CLAIDHEAMH SOLUIS	———

1949

March:	THE BUGLE IN THE BLOOD	... *Bryan MacMahon*
April:	ALL SOULS' NIGHT	... *Joseph Tomelty*
October:	ASK FOR ME TOMORROW	... *Ralph Kennedy*

1950

April:	DESIGN FOR A HEADSTONE	... *Seamus Byrne*
August:	MOUNTAIN FLOOD	... *Jack P. Cunningham*
October:	THE GOLDFISH IN THE SUN	... *Donal Giltinan*

1951

February:	HOUSE UNDER GREEN SHADOWS	*Maurice G. Meldon*
September:	THE DEVIL A SAINT WOULD BE	*Louis D'Alton*
October:	WINDOW ON THE SQUARE	... *Anne Daly*
November:	INNOCENT BYSTANDER	... *Seamus Byrne*

1952

March: THE GENTLE MAIDEN   ... *Donal Giltinan*

July: HOME IS THE HERO   ... *Walter Macken*

1953

January: THE WOOD OF THE WHISPERING *M. J. Molloy*

June: THIS OTHER EDEN   ... *Louis D'Alton*

September: THE PADDY PEDLAR   ... *M. J. Molloy*

1954

January: THE HALF-MILLIONAIRE   ... *John O'Donovan*

February: JOHN COURTNEY ...   ... *John Malone*

March: TWENTY YEARS A-WOOING *John McCann*

July: KNOCKNAVAIN   ...   ... *J. M. Doody*

                A RIVERSIDE CHARADE   ... *Bryan Guinness*

November: IS THE PRIEST AT HOME? ... *Josephy Tomelty*

1955

July: BLOOD IS THICKER THAN WATER *John McCann*

September: THE WILL AND THE WAY   ... *M. J. Molloy*

October: THE LAST MOVE ...   ... *Pauline Maguire*

November: TWILIGHT OF A WARRIOR   ... *Walter Macken*

1. Coffee Palace, 6 Townsend Street : The Ormonde Dramatic Society. W. G. Fay's Comedy Combination, 1891-1899.

2. Antient Concert Rooms, Brunswick Street (now Pearse Street) : Irish Literary Theatre, 1899 ; Irish National Dramatic Co., 1902.

3. The Abbey Theatre, 1904-1951.

4. The Queen's Theatre, Pearse Street present home of Abbey Theatre.

5. Father Mathew Hall : Ormonde Dramatic Society, 1891.

6. Molesworth Hall : Ormonde Dramatic Society 1892-3-7; Irish National Theatre Society, 1903-4 ; Theatre of Ireland, 1910.

7. St. Teresa's Hall, Clarendon Street : W. G. Fay's Irish National Dramatic Company, 1902.

8. 34 Lower Camden Street : The Irish National Theatre Society, 1902.

9. Dun Emer Hall, Hardwicke Street : Theatre of Ireland, 1911-16. ; Irish Theatre, 1915.

10. The Rotunda : W. G. Ormonde's Combination, 1891 ; Theatre of Ireland, 1907.

11. 82 Merrion Square (Home of W. B. Yeats).

12. Abbey Bar, better known as Tommy Lennon's. The Abbey Theatre had no liquor licence, so this neighbouring bar became almost an annexe of the theatre itself.

13. Peacock Theatre (the experimental stage of the Abbey Theatre, and first home of the Gate Theatre).

14. Guinness Memorial Hall : A temporary resting place of the Abbey company after the fire of 1951.

15. Gaiety Theatre : Irish Literary Theatre, 1901.

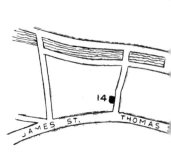

1956

January:	THE BIG BIRTHDAY	... *Hugh Leonard*
July:	EARLY AND OFTEN	... *John McCann*
August:	STRANGE OCCURRENCE ON IRELAND'S EYE ...	... *Denis Johnston*
October:	THE QUARE FELLA	... *Brendan Behan*
November:	WINTER WEDDING	... *Tomás MacAnna*

1957

January:	A LEAP IN THE DARK	... *Hugh Leonard*
February:	WAITING NIGHT ...	... *P. S. Laughlin*
March:	CEAD FEADHA SÍOS (One-Act)	... *Labhras MacBrádaigh*
April:	THE FLYING WHEEL	... *Donal Giltinan*
July:	THE LESS WE ARE TOGETHER	*John O'Donovan*
October:	THE WANTON TIDE	... *Niall Carroll*
November:	GIVE ME A BED OF ROSES	*John McCann*
December:	MUIREANN AGUS AN PRIONNSA	*Pantomime*

1958

February:	POTA AN ANRAITH *(One-Act)*	*W. B. Yeats.*
March:	LOOK IN THE LOOKING GLASS	*Walter Macken*
	AN OIGHREACHT *(One-Act)* ...	*Risteard de Paor*
	CAFFLIN' JOHNNY ...	... *Louis D'Alton*
	IOSAGÁN *(One-Act)* ...	... *Pádraig MacPiarais*
April:	SEVEN MEN AND A DOG	... *Niall Sheridan*
May:	THE SCYTHE AND THE SUNSET	*Denis Johnston*

INDEX